JUST WHEN I THOUGHT I'D HEARD EVERYTHING!

CHARLES GRODIN

JUST WHEN I THOUGHT I'D HEARD EVERYTHING!

Humorous Observations on Life in America

"A First Rate Storyteller"

New York Times

"A Natural Born Raconteur"

Newsweek

ISBN #9780970449993

Illustrations courtesy OpenClipArt.org

Homina Publishing
PO Box 248, Santa Monica, CA 90406
www.hominapublishing.com

TABLE OF CONTENTS

[5]

FOOD AND DRINK

"Cranky has never been my thing."

When I go out for dinner I like to have a glass of wine.

I really don't know anything about wine. So the other night, when I was out for dinner and asked for a glass of wine, when the waiter wanted to know if I wanted one that was balanced or full bodied, I really didn't know what to say. I asked him what the difference was. He said "The full bodied jumps out at you, and the balanced is smoother with more after taste." I still wasn't sure what to say, so I just asked him to bring me what he would order. Later he came by to ask how it was. I said it was fine and asked if it was the balanced or the full bodied? He said "Both." He referred to it as a safety net wine. No matter what the subject, safety nets always seem like a good idea.

I went into a liquor store recently and the liquor store guy seemed to know *everything* about wine. He referred to the different bottles as "this guy," and "this fella over here." And then followed that up with descriptions of the bouquet, the amount of time to let it breathe, the after taste, the thickness – none of which I could possibly remember without taking notes. He told me so many things about the different guys and fellas, I felt like I was an executive with a professional sports team getting prepped on an upcoming draft of the fellas and guys. I wonder if the liquor store person were a woman, she'd say "This girl, and that young lady over there."

The other day I think I learned something I should have known a long time ago. I was feeling uncharacteristically down. I couldn't put my finger on exactly why, and then I realized it was mid-afternoon, and I hadn't eaten anything. Some people get cranky, when they haven't eaten. Cranky has never been my thing. Don't get me wrong. I have a lot of things, but cranky is not one of them. I should have known, but didn't, that you can be down, if you haven't eaten. That may be obvious to most of you, but it wasn't to me, so in case there's anyone out there like me, have something to eat before mid-afternoon.

Of course, we can argue about everything. There was a dispute over who ate the most hot dogs on the fourth of July. Was it the Japanese phenomenon Takeru Kobayashi or his arch rival,

Joey Chestnut? Kobayashi is locked in an ongoing legal battle with Major League Eating over a contract dispute (what else is new?), so he was forbidden from competing in the Annual Coney Island Eating Contest, where Joey Chestnut rules.

Kobayashi wolfed down his dogs at another location. There is also a dispute over just how many dogs Kobayashi ate. Some observers say sixty nine. Some say sixty five. This was all done in ten minutes. What I found missing from the reporting is, if you eat over sixty hot dogs in ten minutes – just *how* sick do you get?

There's a new study out that confirms what diet experts have been saying for years. If you eat slowly, you're more likely to eat less. They say fast eaters use a large utensil, eat as quickly as possible and don't even pause between bites. They say slow eaters use a small utensil, take small bites, chew food between fifteen and twenty times and put their utensil down between bites.

It all makes a lot of sense, unless you're out with my brother-in-law. Don't get me wrong. My brother-in-law is a great guy – really good looking and as slim as anyone would want to be, but he's a *slow* eater. He may be the slowest eater in America, I don't know about other countries, but in America, no question.

I mean he not only takes small bites, chews his food thoroughly, he also puts his utensil down for *long* periods of time *between* bites. I had dinner with him and some other relatives recently. After a few hours I graciously (I hope) said goodnight to my brother-in-law and the others and went home. I wouldn't be shocked to hear he's still there taking small bites and chewing slowly. I'm sure eating slowly is better than eating fast, but there's only so many hours in a day, and I can't spend nine of them eating.

I like Japanese food. I've enjoyed it for years, particularly sushi, which I buy at the market. I am considerably less enthusiastic about going to Japanese restaurants, because inevitably the people suggesting I go want to sit at one of those hibachi grills, where they cook everything in front of you. I don't have a problem with the food being cooked in front of me.

I *do* have a problem with the chef flipping the knives around. I've never heard of anyone accidentally getting stabbed at one of the Hibachi grills, but there's always a first. Even if it never would happen, it's on my mind. I don't know about you, but *my* appetite isn't particularly helped by wondering if one of the chefs' knives is going to slip out of his hand and *stab* me.

I'm not exactly sure why they automatically serve you a wedge of lemon on the side of your glass, if you order a Coke, for example. That's *without* asking. Various things I order, they ask if you'd like them to grind pepper on it. That – I get, but lemon is getting right up there with pepper. Lemon on the side of a glass of Pepsi is a given, but the other day I ordered some turkey soup, and the waiter asked if I'd like some lemon squeezed in it. After I was sure he wasn't kidding, I just said "No thanks." Lemon in turkey soup?!

I saw an interview on television recently with a hundred and six year old man, who goes to work every day on Wall Street at the stock market. He was sitting down for the interview, and he seemed quite intelligent, as he described the stock market around the time of the crash. He said he had two sons in their seventies, who had retired. I didn't see the interview from the beginning, so I don't know if the following questions were asked. What do you eat? Do you exercise? How do you spend your free time? Working at a hundred and six?! This man has to know *something* most of us don't.

Years ago I went out to dinner in New York with my wife and teenage son. When my son gave his order, the waiter looked at him for a moment then said "Not possible." We were all confused for a second and realized he meant no one, not even a teenager could eat that much. I said "Well, what if we take home what he can't finish?" Without missing a beat the waiter said "Most probable." "Not possible. Most probable." Not only was the food good, but we had a good laugh *and* some good leftovers.

I'm big on taking home part of my dinner or lunch when at a restaurant. I don't plan the take home. I just *never* get around to finishing a whole – whatever. When I was a kid, I never saw food being thrown out, and the lesson stuck. Most people are fine with take home, but recently I had lunch with an Englishman, and I never *saw* an eyebrow go so high, as the Englishman's, when I told the waiter I'd take the rest home, but old habits die hard if ever, no matter how high someone's eyebrow is raised.

One of the most interesting things about life is we never stop learning. I was in a chocolate store the other day, and I was surprised to see they sell chocolate crosses. Even though they were out of them, they also sell chocolate Star of David's and chocolate menorahs. I found all of that pretty surprising, and if that wasn't enough they told me the chocolate religious symbols outsell the item right next to them – the chocolate lambs. Would you eat a chocolate cross, a chocolate Star of David or a chocolate menorah? I wouldn't. Personally I'm not even comfortable eating the chocolate lamb. I stay with the sugar free chocolate with almonds. The less provocative my chocolate, the better.

HE*A*LTH

"Power naps and other efforts."

What would you do if you were walking down the street – you looked up – and saw a dog falling from a ledge off a window on the fourth floor of a building? Not a puppy. A medium sized dog. David Quinton said when his *wife* looked up and saw the dog about to fall – she couldn't stand it. That certainly motivated Mr. Quinton to hold his arms out and catch the dog. The dog was fine. Dave Quinton got a knee injury. He said he was happy it wasn't a Great Dane, or he'd be crippled.

I was driving down a major road the other day, and I saw a sign that said Falling Rock Zone. What?! What am *I* supposed to do if a big falling rock – a boulder comes falling down and smashes into my car as well as me. Here's a suggestion. Save the money on the signs and use it to stop rocks from falling on us.

I was recently having teeth pain, and at the same time learned that my regular dentist is not covered by my insurance, so I got a list of a number of dentists in my area, who do take my insurance, and I chose one. Big mistake. He took x-rays and had his hygienist do about thirty minutes of probing my gums. He then gave me a prescription for Penicillin and said that he'd see me in a couple of weeks.

The pain got *much* worse after I saw him, so I went to my regular dentist. He took x-rays and said I needed a root canal. In other words, the first dentist had the white jacket, but was he really a dentist? I mean I didn't see any certificates. His name wasn't even on the door! The lesson: don't go to *any* so called medical person without a recommendation from someone you trust.

I saw an article recently about a new book that was advising people to gain weight, as they grew older. It *wasn't* a joke. I'd like to know the percentage of people, who *don't* gain weight, as they get older. I would bet it's less than 10%, and *that* group are work out fanatics – a *small* group. We should *try* to gain weight, as we get older? I don't *think* so. An *effort* is *not* necessary.

I went to the eye doctor the other day. I got a good report. At one point as part of the examination, the doctor, a lovely woman put drops in my eyes to dilute them. She started to explain to me what was going on – eye wise – something I have no interest in hearing. I don't want to see my heart on a t.v. screen either.

It's not just medical. I don't want to hear the plumber's explanation either. *They* know. Why do *I* have to? I have other things on my mind. What's, I guess, for better or worse *different* about me, while my eyes dilute, I *tell* them what's on *my* mind. After all, I *am* the customer.

Tomorrow is Thanksgiving. First of all, I'm thankful that my family and I appear to be in good health, although a few years ago during a routine physical checkup, my doctor couldn't really feel what he's supposed to feel when he put his hands on the side of my neck. He sent me to a special guy who checks your *carotid artery*, I think they call it.

That's the one that carries the blood to the brain. That guy hooked me up to a special machine and as a nurse ran the tests, every time she moved whatever she had on my neck, there was a swooshing sound "swoosh." Sometimes she moved it, and there *wasn't* a swoosh, and that really got my attention. I chose not to ask her what was going on. I'm sure I was afraid of her answer.

I never took my eyes off her face! Her expression seemed to say "Uh oh, I don't like what I'm seeing here." Later the doctor told me I was absolutely *fine*, and you weren't *supposed* to hear "swoosh" every time they moved the neck thing. I wish he'd have mentioned that, before I got hooked up.

This is from the New York Times. Evidently there's some new hormone researchers have just discovered that sharply reduces the desire to eat. So far they've just tried it on mice, and it evidently sends a signal to the mouse's brain that says "Eat less" and the mouse eats less. The scientists at Stanford University discovered it. It's evidently made in the stomach and the small intestine. I'm certain you'd have to go to medical school to know how you spot it. Mice given the hormone for eight days ate half as much as usual. It apparently slows the passage of food through the stomach – of course, slowing down *when* you might next feel hungry.

This has only been tested on mice, but drug companies are scrambling to come up with a way to get it to humans, since our obesity rates are sky rocketing. An obesity researcher from the University of Washington said "The chance that this is going to hold up in humans is very high!" However, another obesity expert from the University of Cincinnati says the effect of body weight seems to be *subtle*. He means the mouse's body weight. Not only that, but the mice might be losing *muscle* weight. If we could get a pill that would make us eat less, without our left arm eventually falling off, that would be good.

I'm sure we could get a pill for everything, but when you read the potential side effects for just about everything we might take – it has to give you pause. I'm told drug companies have to report something even if it happened once, but we're not told that – just what *could* happen, not the *odds* it will. I want to hear the odds.

Otherwise I'm not taking it. Of course, the mice don't get to read the side effects *or* the odds.

I've heard of power lunches, power dinners, but the other day I think for the first time for me anyway – I heard the term power nap. I was at some event honoring a couple of people, and one of the guys was a *really* high achiever. If I heard right, he was actually on the radio every day in two different cities – *live*. So in between all that running to airports and being *in* the air and *on* the air – somewhere in there – he took a power nap. A nap I guess that's supposed to give you more power or at least more energy – I guess. I don't know… lately I've found myself taking about a nap a week, and when I wake up I feel more rested but not really more energetic and certainly not more powerful. I'm not really sure what a power nap is.

The other day I noticed I was uncharacteristically edgy. Then I realized there was this loud pulsating music on the radio. I shut it off, and immediately became my non nervous self. Sometimes it's good when you don't feel exactly right to shut something off or maybe turn something on, whatever – change something, and I don't mean your tie, although sometimes it *could* be your tie.

In England scientist Gerald Lincoln told the BBC Radio's Today program that *men* get bad tempered, emotional and depressed, because they are suffering from irritable *male* syndrome. So it's a hormonal thing for *men* as well as women. With *men* it's a lack of testosterone that causes the problems, and a *shot* of testosterone can make previously withdrawn men more *energetic*, more *motivated* and, of course, more interested in sex.

It seems to me that generally speaking for *men* the bad tempered, irritable thing comes more with age, so now they're saying a *shot* can take care of that. Since we are also now hearing about *Botox* getting rid of wrinkles, the time may be right around the corner where a lot of angry *old* looking guys are going to be turning into a lot of *happy young* looking guys. Isn't science wonderful?

There are certain things I remember from childhood that will never go away. "Don't leave lights on in a room you're not in. Do you want to make the electric company rich?" Or "The electric company has enough money without you helping them." I also remember being edgy about keeping the refrigerator door open too long.

Again, I think that was about contributing to the electric company, or maybe it was because stuff would melt or spoil, I'm not sure. I can only tell you I became pretty quick in getting in and out of that refrigerator. Don't drip water on the floor was another one. It was the kitchen floor which was covered with linoleum, and what's a couple of drops of water going to do to linoleum anyway? For whatever reason, I never asked, I just tried as hard as I could not to drip water on the floor.

At the top of the list no question were rules about cleanliness, keeping the house clean, keeping yourself clean, actually keeping everything clean. "Don't track mud into the house" didn't have to be said more than once. "Wash your hands" was another obvious one. Wash your hands before or after everything you can think of, and I did. I still do, *plenty*.

But now a recent story in the New York Daily News stopped me in my tracks. "Dirt does a body good, health pros say." Some experts are now saying that a certain amount of dirt is good, that if we're washing up too much we could be weakening our immune systems killing as the experts put it "helpful germs and spurring the growth of mutant strains of superbacteria." One expert said "If you're bacteria, you're not just going to sit down and give up. You're going to develop new forms."

Of course the people who manufacture soap and other antibacterial products disagree. They insist you can never be too clean. They say there's no proof all this washing up leads to stronger bacteria. My whole life I've been dedicated to staying as clean as possible, and now this. When I read the story, I considered both sides, then I thought about what my mother would say. I put the newspaper down and washed my hands.

When I was ten years old, I was impeached as president of my 5th grade class for as the teacher put it "Talking incessantly." I asked what incessantly meant? She said "Look it up in the dictionary." I did. It said "Talk without cease." Recently for the first time in my life, I lost my voice. I got a sore throat. Normally if that ever happens I lay low, and it goes away, but there were two events scheduled, where I was expected to and wanted to show up. The second event, all on the same day, I *was* the speaker with *laryngitis*. At the end of that night, I lost my voice. I lost it for a couple of days. I noticed, probably like anyone else, if you can't talk you tend to *think* more – and who needs *that*? Some people, in my opinion, don't think *enough*, but some of us like *me, already* think too much *without* laryngitis. So actually it wasn't the pain of the sore throat that bothered me, it was all that extra *thinking*.

Recently I heard about a study that said we should all be exercising an hour a day. It didn't interest me. Here's why. It was about thirty years ago I was having dinner with this friend of mine, who looked as though he'd been working out a lot. He told me about a trainer he'd run into in the gym, and this guy had really whipped him into shape.

He gave me his number, and eventually the trainer started to work me out *an hour a day*. I really felt he was pushing me too hard, so in an effort to slow him down, I'd say things like "Hey, I'm not going to try out for the Olympics." He always acted as though I hadn't spoken and kept driving me. Eventually he drove me right into the hospital, because I couldn't walk or even stand up. I had a full recovery without surgery, but the idea of exercising an hour a day has never been enticing again. Twenty minutes a day *without* that trainer in the room seems more like it. Of course, I don't do that either.

It feels as though every year or so the government comes out with these guidelines for our health. Recently they suggested something like eat eight servings of fruit and vegetables a day. *What?!* If I did that, I'd have no room for anything *but* fruit and vegetables. Goodbye steak. Goodbye chops. I appreciate the government's good intentions, and I'm sure they're right, but they don't say anything about actually enjoying your life, while you're eating all these fruits and vegetables.

I think it's very important to be goal oriented. If you have a goal it's a very good way to get your focus off yourself – which is always a good idea. I'm extremely goal oriented, but sometimes I think I go too far. If I see the garbage has to be taken out, I'll take it out, even if I think it's *so* heavy, it will hurt my lower back. I do it, and my lower back tightens up. Happens all the time. I have this slant board I lie on that stretches out your lower back. The other day at the same moment I was heading toward the slant board, I felt I was ready to write a commentary, I'd been thinking about for a few days. What to do? Instead of waiting ten minutes, I wrote the commentary while lying on a sixty degree angle on the slant board. That goes beyond goal oriented into compulsion.

I heard a commercial for Flomax on television the other day. It's a product that helps, I think, only men with urinary issues. No need to get specific here but after the obligatory listing of side effects, the commercial said "Avoid situations where injuries can occur." "Avoid situations where injuries can occur?!" That could mean don't leave the house *or* stay home. And certainly bull fighting, but Flomax or not, I'm *always* trying to avoid situations where injuries may occur.

I'm hearing a lot of commercials on the radio these days for dealing with depression. One came on the other day and said something like "Are you feeling down, kind of anxious, not sleeping as well as you'd like, seem to have lost that get up and go? Well, you may be suffering from Major Depressive Disorder. If you'd like to be a member of a group for study," and then they give a number to call.

I can imagine the call. "Hello, I heard your commercial on Major Depressive Disorder." "Yes, what is your name please?" "Charles Grodin." "Charles Grodin, the guy who was in the movies?" "Yeah, I'm on the radio now." "Are you depressed, Charles?" "Well, y'know the whole World Trade Center anniversary, terrorism, y'know." "Uh huh."

Then I'd ask "Are you a doctor?" "No, I'm just taking the information." I'd then say. "Well, how do *you* feel?" She then says "Well, I'm kind of depressed myself to be honest." "Yes, well thank you very much," and then I'd get off the phone. Personally, I think you need a doctor, if you *don't* feel kind of at least *different* these days.

I think MRI's have gotten a bad rap. I had one recently. They wanted to take a closer look at an ear situation. I found the whole experience – strange as it may seem – *fun*! First of all I don't get out that much, and when I do, I don't like to stay too long. This took thirty minutes. Perfect. You're *not* all enclosed.

You can see the room from a little mirror they angle a certain way on your forehead. I could, whenever I chose, *see* an extremely friendly lady with her hand on my ankle the whole time – a reassuring touch. I've never had a woman put her hand on my ankle that long.

You hear a lot of weird sounds, but I was just thinking about what instruments I'd add to make that a possible commercial melody. It *must* be disclosed that I had no symptoms, so not surprisingly it turned out I had nothing to worry about, so that probably put a positive spin on the MRI in the first place. There were actually *two* very friendly women in the room. I mean how bad can that be? All in all; a *very* enjoyable experience.

I have a lot of friends who golf. I don't golf. I have friends who bowl. I've bowled, but I wouldn't say I *bowl*. Almost every one of these friends have injuries from their golfing and bowling – mostly golfing. These are nagging long term injuries. These friends are always trying to get me to golf or bowl – get out there,

[29]

an activity, but I have an unusual high awareness
of their nagging injuries.

I don't have any nagging injuries. I watch what
I eat. I'll have a drink, but I don't abuse alcohol.
There's an interesting phrase alcohol abuse.
Why don't they call it self-abuse? The *alcohol's*
not being abused, because you're drinking it. In
other words I'm not interested in being fat, sick
from drinking or having nagging injuries.

A friend of mine went on a long mountain hike
recently. Of course, he now has some kind of
knee injury. Obviously, I'm not interested in
mountain hikes. To each his own, but maybe you
people out there with all those nagging injuries
ought to give more thought to what you're
doing. Now don't get me wrong. It's not like I
don't have at least my share of problems. There
just not nagging injuries.

I got one of those little bottles that I think are
kind of new on the market that say you can get
rid of 99.9% of any germs on your hands by
rubbing this liquid on. I got it, so if I'm out for
dinner and someone comes over and shakes my
hand, when they're gone, I can discretely use my
99.9% thing. I'm certain they're not saying

100% get rids of germs but only 99.9% in the event of that possible law suit -- "Hey, we never said 100%!" I can see a day, when we're more like the folks in Japan – no hand shaking – just a lot of bowing, or better yet – just a pat on the back.

Because of a flair-up of an old back injury, I was on the phone with the doctor the other day. He told me to exercise for ten minutes a day and twenty to thirty minutes three times a week on my stationery bike for aerobics. I translate twenty to thirty minutes to eighteen. Sue me! As we said goodbye, he said "The exercise releases the endorphins." "Good," I thought. "It's good to release endorphins." I've known that for years.

The next day I realized I didn't actually know what endorphins were, so I looked it up in the dictionary. Amazingly to me anyway, the word wasn't there, and it wasn't a tiny dictionary either. Research revealed that endorphins were only discovered in 1975. That gets my old dictionary off the hook. Research also revealed that releasing endorphins can reduce pain, reduce stress and can even slow down the aging process. The *really* good news is in addition to

exercise, endorphins can *also* be released
through massage, laughter and sex, and only *one*
of those can get you in trouble.

A man was with his wife in the delivery room,
where she was about to give birth. He's asked to
hold her hand, while they gave her an epidural
shot to ease the pain. He passed out and suffered
a head injury, and the couple sued. Is this
grounds for a suit? I don't know.

I also don't know, if he watched the needle go in
his wife *causing* him to pass out, or his stress
just came from being in the middle of it all. I do
know this. I was there when my wife gave birth
to our son, but the doctors did all the hands on
stuff. I never watch needles go in, or when I'm
at the doctor's, I decline to watch whatever
organs of mine they have up on a t.v. screen.
They always ask me if I want to see, and I
always say "No, that's alright." I've never
passed out either. Know thyself.

I was out to dinner years ago with former New
York Met Manger, Bobby Valentine and his
father in law former great Brooklyn Dodger
pitcher Ralph Branca. Bobby looked
tremendous. I asked him if he worked out. He

[32]

said he did – an hour a day. I asked Ralph if he worked out. Ralph was pushing ninety. He said he didn't, but he felt he was making progress, because he *thought* about working out recently. Hey! It's a beginning!

Probably the most common experience we all have is we know what it's like to have a problem in a relationship. It really doesn't matter what kind of relationship it is. You have a relationship? You're going to have some problems. Second only to problems in relationships, as a sure thing, are back problems.

Whoever first got the idea that we should stop walking on all fours probably made a mistake. I've dealt with back problems ever since I had a trainer I've mentioned, who mistakenly thought he was getting me ready for the Olympics. Over the years I've had shots, pills, a trainer (a new one), a masseuse, a chiropractor, jacuzzis, kind of lying upside down on a slant board...it's all helped. Generally speaking in recent times I've done very well in the back pain department.

About a week ago during a flair-up, I asked a chiropractor "Hey, what causes all this anyway?" I hadn't been doing any heavy lifting or even sudden twists and turns.

He said he felt just about every one of his patients were there because of stress. Stress! Of course, I forgot! So what do you do about stress? There's a book on this, but one smart friend said "Think about what might be causing the stress. Probably you're not experiencing some emotion. You're stuffing it, and it's going right into your back!" It's true.

If I'm mad about something I tend not to think about it, because I don't want to walk around mad, but if the choice is walking around in pain, or maybe not even being *able* to walk around, I *guess* I should walk around mad. I guess…

Yesterday after getting up *very* early and working all day (working for *me* is sitting in a Stratolounger and writing). Anyway after working all day, I suddenly found myself kicking back in the chair, closing my eyes, and if not exactly dozing off – *trying* to doze off. As I was *trying* to doze, I thought "Hmm, this is something new for me – dozing off." So after about a minute of trying to doze, I decided I could write a commentary about dozing off instead of actually dozing.   For some of us dozing off is a little tougher than it is for others.

At what age is it normal to walk into a room and forget why you came in? You know it's to get something or do something – but what? I'm in my seventies, and it never really phases me when it happens, because I know it's not unusual.

I've asked people in their fifties, and they say it's not unusual for them either. I haven't checked, but I bet it's not *that* unusual for some people in their forties either. If you're in your thirties, and it regularly happens, I'd get it checked out. I say all this, because it's also not unusual for me to talk to people who forget why they came into a room and get *worried.* Don't worry. It's not unusual.

I was in a dentist's chair recently for two hours. I had been led to believe I'd be there for ten minutes – *tops*. From now on when I get into a dentist's chair I'm going to ask "Approximately how long do you think this will be?" I'll ask politely – I promise you. I think it's better if you *know* how long something is – plays, movies etc. – not *life* – *definitely* not life. All I could think of during my two hours was I've got to come up with a good line, as I leave. Here's the line. "I think there's been a misunderstanding. *I* thought I was coming here for a free pack of sugarless gum." If *you* like it – use it.

I have an every single day ongoing theme in my life. I think about it and talk about it every day I'm sure to some degree of annoyance from my family anyway, because that's who I'm mostly around. The theme is in the form of a question. The question is what am I missing? What can I do to live as smart a life as I can? I think of things all the time.

The other day I thought of something to live smarter that *I* was really annoyed at myself that it took me so long to think of it. I've often talked about how I'm blessed with unusually good health.

Neither I nor my family can even *remember* me being sick, but I was sick recently. Everyone was shocked – especially me! If somebody is sick in my house say with a cold, I keep my distance. It's always worked until recently. I started to think – how could I have been smarter and avoided this cold? Surgical masks!

[36]

Doctors are always around sick contagious people, and when they are, they wear a surgical mask. I got one for everybody in my house, and I suggest you do too – to use when needed. Surgical masks! You'll be glad you did! Of course, I'm the only one in my house that has ever worn it. I'm also the only one in my house who *never* gets a cold. In fairness, it probably helps that I rarely go anywhere.

That recent story in the news about the man who was impersonating a dentist got my attention. This pretend dentist while attempting to pull a tooth pulled *half* of it. I've never seen a profession where every time I or others go to a new dentist, the new guy will take a look and say "Who did *that* filling?"

MANNERS

"I'll take a warm hi any day."

A recent survey conducted by LetsTalk.com revealed 66% of those surveyed felt it was fine to be on your cell phone in a supermarket. 45% said alright on public transportation. 21% thought it was o.k. in a restaurant. 2% said o.k. in movies or the theatre and *38%* said o.k. in a *bathroom.* I'm sure they mean *public* as well as private bathrooms.

I *say* don't do it *anywhere,* unless it's an emergency. O.k. I'll concede the market to let your wife or husband know what soups they have. It's o.k. in the *movies* or *theatre?* The 2% who said that are *certifiable!* Recently a friend of mine was in a store where a woman was talking loudly on her cell phone. Another person came into the store whom my friend knew, and they began to chat. The woman on her cell *shooshed* her.

There was a big hullabaloo about the great football receiver Randy Moss mooning the opposing team's fans. Even though Randy kept his pants *on* for the moon – a moon is a moon. For those of you who possibly might not know –

generally you moon by at *least* slightly bending over and facing your tush in the direction of the object of the moon.

I thought the criticism of Randy's moon was justified, *until* I read that *earlier* the opposing team's *fans* mooned Randy and his team, when their bus entered the parking lot. The report didn't say whether the fans had kept their pants on. Whatever – I'm on Randy's side on this one. An eye for an eye. A moon for a moon.

There's so many things I know little or nothing about. One of them is design. You don't want me to be your decorator, however, I do have a strong opinion about white, tan or any light colored rugs. First there's either a sign up, or the host or hostess will ask you to take off your shoes, as you enter their house.

Then the person who chose to have such a light colored rug is always seeing a spot, they have to clean in between the on-going instruction to take off your shoes. Please! Stop with the light colored rugs. Leave us civilians alone. We have enough problems.

I've been fortunate to be friends with the brilliant song writer, singer Paul Simon for a long time. His songs, are of course, memorable, *Sounds of Silence, Bridge Over Troubled Water* and countless more. We recently had lunch and I was reminded that sometimes he will very casually say something that just sticks in your mind, not the biggest surprise in the world. As we were chatting, he observed "Let me look at my schedule, and I'll get back to you on that," is the new *no*.

I'm not saying telephones are driving me crazy – but close. Talking on cell phones while you're disturbing others -- holding a cell phone while driving – not *insanity* – but close. Endless conversations with recordings. Endless waits on hold, while they tell you how important you call is to them and what a wonderful company they are?! Please! *Stop!* Give me a break. I think we gave up too soon on carrier pigeons.

People *must* understand that "how ya' doin'?" is almost always a greeting not a question. I was filling my car with gas in a gas station recently, and a man I don't know, came out to me and asked "How ya' doin'?" I assume from what followed, he owned the station. After we greeted each other, he went on to tell me in *great detail* what was going on with his station and the gas company. It was incredibly detailed, and you would have to be in that field to follow it at all, so I, of course, had no idea what he was saying.

I politely nodded for what felt like a very long time and then began to slowly inch away in my car. He *followed* me with *more* details. Again "How ya' doin'" to a *stranger* anyway is overwhelmingly a greeting; not a question.

A woman wrote to an advice columnist recently about whether she should have waited to eat her salad, while her friends were still at the salad bar. There were other women sitting at the table, who seemed to be waiting, but it seems they weren't *having* salad and were waiting for soup.

One woman at her table seemed to take umbrage that this woman *wasn't* eating her salad, even though she wasn't having soup. The advice columnist said to eat or *not* eat would be o.k. I can't even follow all of this, but it reminds me of the time years ago, when I was having lunch with the late actor Charles Bronson.

It was at Universal Studios, and there were five
of us in the booth. Mr. Bronson, some of you
will remember appeared to be a very tough guy
on the screen. He appeared that way *off* screen
as well. That day at lunch his food came first,
and he dug right in.

After a few minutes, I looked at him, and as a
joke said "Why don't you start?" He wasn't
amused. He looked at me for what felt like a
very long moment and said "Y'know if I have a
problem with someone I don't hit them or
anything like that. I just *bite* their jugular vein."
He seemed serious. I wonder what an advice
columnist would say about *that*? Probably
"Always leave Mr. Bronson alone."

I was at work once, when I passed a colleague in
the hall, and he said to me in kind of a
complaining tone "When I saw you before I said
"Hello," and you said "Hey." I wasn't sure if he
was kidding or he was actually offended, but I
said I consider "Hey" friendlier than "Hello" or
even "Hi."

He said "You consider "Hey" friendlier than
"Hi?"" I said "Absolutely. I say "Hey" to my

closest friends. If I said "Hello," they'd think something was wrong." He nodded, and we went our separate ways. The whole experience reminded me how easily we can offend each other. Even in these stressful times of searching for weapons of mass destruction, a "Hey" can cause trouble.

The other day at the market a woman walked toward me with a big smile on her face and *so* warmly said "Hi!" Even though I didn't recognize her, I returned her greeting with a warm "Hi" of my own.

Then she walked by and greeted someone behind me. Maybe I should have been embarrassed, but I wasn't. It's so nice to see that kind of genuine warmth these days, my enjoyment of it overcame any embarrassment I might have felt. In other words, even if it's not intended for me, I'll take a warm hi any day.

Once at an event in New York, I found myself alone with the Duchess of Gloucester, who is the cousin of the Queen of England. We looked at each other. Neither of us could think of anything to say. Finally I asked "What is the

[45]

main focus of your life?" She looked at me as though I had just pinched her tush.

After an *extremely* uncomfortable silence, she said "My family." There was another long silence, and then she said "I wouldn't ask *you* such a question, but since you asked me, "What is the main focus of *your* life?" I said "My family." Amazingly the world didn't come to an end.

I've never gotten used to the accepted idea that at the end of each day at the New York Stock Exchange people stand high above the trading floor and applaud. I'm not sure if the traders down below are applauding. I can't imagine those who had bad *trading* days are.

Recently I appeared at the Nasdaq Stock Exchange with other people on behalf of a charity. At some point everyone all around me was applauding. I asked another person, who was there for the charity and applauding "Exactly why is everyone applauding?" He didn't seem to know either, but we guessed it was the end of another day of trading.

I don't get it, but I didn't want to be rude, so I applauded. If you work in an office, somewhere, do you all applaud at the end of the day? I mean I realize people want to go home – I just really don't get the applause thing. This all came to mind recently when I saw members of the House of Representatives *applauding* that they passed a *non binding resolution* against the president sending more troops to Iraq. I even heard some cheers over passage of this *non-binding* resolution. I guess applauding and cheering just makes people feel good. I guess.

This past summer, because we had some family and friends visiting, I got out more to restaurants and the theatre, and I came to the conclusion that I wish dinner or a show would last no longer than an hour and a half. To keep the peace, I might go to an hour forty five, but honestly, give me that hour and a half at the table or at the theatre. This could be a male/female thing.

I hope I'm not coming off sexist, if I say women seem to be more comfortable sitting than men. You ladies could take that as a compliment, that women have more patience. When I told my brother my thoughts on this he said "Yeah, well, you've always been more edgy than most

[47]

people." I said "I prefer *restless* to edgy," but he said "No edgy." I think there're a lot of us edgy men around. Sometimes when the dinner drags on past my hour and a half cut off point, and I'm out in the parking lot hanging around near my car, I'll notice another guy or two hanging around near their car. I figure they're fellow hour and a half guys.

I'm not saying I'm right about this, but still I bet there are millions of people who feel as I do. I can't seem to handle the sit down dinner parties where at some point the hostess or host asks everyone to respond to a question. A recent one was "How did you meet your spouse?" No big deal right? It was for me.

I can't really tell you why. I just know as the people around the table dutifully told their spouse meeting stories – first I was silent, then tense, then I started making jokes. Stuff like "I don't believe for a minute, that's how you met him." I graciously, I hope, managed to leave the table before my turn came. I have a pretty good spouse meeting story too. I just didn't feel like sharing it with a group of people – some of whom I barely knew.

Stuff like that I choose to share only with close friends, who probably already *know* how I met my spouse. I think what I just said is fairly defensible, I think, but my behavior recently at a dinner party wasn't. Even though like most of us I have a tendency to be on my side, on this one, even *I* can see I'm out of line. The host asked everyone their thoughts on the election. It wasn't take-your-turn-as-we-go-around-the-table, and it wasn't obligatory, although a few times the host looked at me and said "Chuck?" I again made a joke and then got up, left the room and began to study what was on the walls in another room.

Why am I like this? Does it remind me of school? Maybe. Is it the structure that gets me? I'm not sure. I know this though. As bad as I am with all of the above, if anyone ever starts a game of charades, the sound of tires screeching into the night means Charles has left the building.

I was hired by Roger Ailes in 1994 to have my own show on CNBC which Roger was running at the time. One of the reasons he gave for giving me my own hour show was he felt I had "the gift of gab." A gift of gab is a very good thing to have, if you have your own television or radio program, but even people with their own show *must* remember when off the air for the sake of friends and family -- put a *lid* on it.

For years I've been hearing about the haughty French, the superior, condescending attitude of the French, but since I've never been to France or even hardly ever run into any French people, you couldn't prove it by me.

Recently I wandered into a French restaurant. I didn't even know it was a French restaurant. I just dropped into a place for a cheeseburger on the way to pick up my car at a parking lot.

After saying I'd like a cheeseburger, I said to the waiter, "That's with lettuce, tomato, and raw onion, o.k.?" Since he didn't respond, I repeated myself. When he didn't respond again, I said it a third time. Then he looked at me and said in what I'd have to call a superior, condescending, haughty way "It is a cheeseburger."

I could have said "It's not that obvious, you can cook onions too or you can say hold the lettuce," but I just nodded. I wasn't offended. Actually I thought it was kind of funny, but if I heard that on a regular basis, or even more than once, I'd probably find it at least haughty.

It's always been very important to me to be as friendly as I can be to people, and I believe I've succeeded in doing that. But when I became aware that in a recent conversation with a representative from the phone company, I really had to try hard to live up to my standard, I decided to take stock and try to figure out what had happened. My problem with the phone company really started with the advent of caller I.D. Who wouldn't want caller I.D.?

At a time when just about every other day, the phone rings around dinner time with someone doing a survey about something where they "just want to ask you a few questions" wouldn't you like a name on a screen that warns you not to answer the phone. Like "Such and Such Research" I like to be warned on who's calling.

I'd really appreciate it. Call me too sensitive. I'm fairly private. I don't want to even tell a *stranger* what kind of transportation I use, for example. To set up my caller I.D., very nice people from the phone company began to appear at my house…a lot. They worked in the basement. They worked on the road. They were up in the trees, and after several weeks of this, not only did I *not* have caller I.D., I couldn't even get a *call*. If you called me you'd hear a loud piercing sound, and if I answered *I'd* hear the piercing sound.

The other day a technician who'd done quite a lot of work on trying to get me my caller I.D. called to see how it was working. I tried to very nicely tell him it wasn't working at *all*, that I had talked to several people at his organization, that there was a period there where they told me my problem was I didn't have *privacy plus* in addition to caller I.D. and when I said "Well, give me the privacy plus," the next thing I got was *more* piercing sounds!

The fella on the phone said he'd like to come back out, that he was confident that the problem was…I forget what he said the problem was, because I jumped on his use of the word "confident". I told him I'm sure he and the rest of the gang at the phone company all really *meant* well, but I was just pleased at this point my phone worked at all.

I gave up on all their new caller I.D. privacy plus stuff, and said maybe sometime in the future *they'd* change, maybe consider not selling things, until they work, and then *I'd* change, and we could all be together again. He actually said "Aw, don't give up." I said, "I have to give up for now. Sometimes it's better to just give up." He then actually said, "I humbly apologize." "O.k." I said. "It's just at this point in time, I can't take it anymore," and then I said "Goodbye." We were both nice about it though, which is always important.

I had a cable show on CNBC and then MSNBC for five years. Once I had the television psychologist Sonya Friedman as a guest. She'd had a show on CNN for years called Sonya Live, where she made observations about you and gave you advice. She said I was *avoidant*. What?! "I said I'm not avoidant!" Even though I wasn't 100% sure what avoidant meant.

I later looked avoidant up in the dictionary and it's not listed. It's not an actual word. Anyway... I told Sonya I've had big fights right there on television with Alan Dershowitz, former Senator Alan Simpson from Wyoming or one of those places where there aren't that many people to choose from for whom to vote. She said she was aware of those fights, but she *still* felt I was avoidant.

Then a friend of mine who's known me for 35 years commenting on the Dershowitz/Grodin shouting match said "My God, Chuck would never do anything close to that in life. He's... and I know she didn't say avoidant, but it was close enough.

Personally I don't feel I'm avoidant. I feel I'm a gentleman, and gentlemen don't make *issues* out of things except when absolutely necessary. Anyway that's what I think. I also think avoidant *should* be a word. I would *put* it in the dictionary and define it as a compliment – "people who avoid conflict unless absolutely necessary."

When the allergy season is in full blossom an important question comes up for those of us who try to be top of the line polite. If someone sneezes – say five times in say about eight seconds, are you supposed to say Bless you eight times? Bless you. Bless you. Bless you. Bless you. Bless you. Bless you. Bless you. Bless you. Or should you wait a bit and come in with one "bless you" at the end of the five sneezes? The dilemma is what if it's only one sneeze, and there you are silently waiting for more sneezes. Couldn't you appear somewhat rude, as the sneezer looks at you. Nothing's easy.

I read a report from the Associated Press, that the American Dental Association for the first time has allowed its seal of approval to appear on gum, specifically Wrigley's sugar free gums Orbit, Extra and Eclipse. The report says that those three gums have been shown to help prevent cavities, reduce plaque and strengthen teeth. The report also says that the Dental Association's studies were partially *funded* by the Wrigley Company.

Usually that would make me wary, but *I've* been chewing those gums for years. I'm not saying strangers stop me on the street to comment on my teeth and gums, but I do get an excellent report from my dentist, so I tend to believe what they say about the sugarless Wrigley, Orbit, Extra and Eclipse and in my experience sugar free gum *not* made by Wrigley as well.

I'm also compelled to say I don't chew gum in public or even in the privacy of where I live in front of others. Living with me is enough of a challenge without me chewing in your presence, even if my gum is sugar free.

The other day I read a story about a baseball player who has an injured hand. He said he could play through the pain, but when someone in an airport gave him a really strong handshake recently, it was incredibly painful. The story reminded me how much I and I'm sure many of you dislike *really* strong handshakes.

They can hurt, even if you *don't* have an injured hand. All you men out there, and I'm sure it's almost always men, who *give* these really strong handshakes – please re-think them. Maybe it *doesn't* show how strong or amazingly sincere you are. Maybe it just suggests you're trying too hard to prove *something*. Lighten up on the shakes!

I was at a restaurant the other night, when everyone at a table across the room began to sing happy birthday to someone. When the song was finished I was struck by how many people in the place joined in the song and the applause.

It was the *amount* of strangers and the *extent* of the singing and applause that got my attention. Of course I could be wrong, but I thought to myself – *finally* here's something we can *all* agree on – applauding someone's birthday. At a time when we seem *so* divided over so many things – it felt like a *particularly* nice moment. Then I realized that might not be what happened at *all*. Maybe the people in the restaurant *didn't* feel a special need to unite over *something*. *Maybe* they just had a lot to drink.

Recently, I was with a small group of people, and there was the most talkative person I'd ever seen there. She said she knew she talked a lot, but if anyone wanted to jump right in, she'd show she could be a big listener too, but, of course, when you're around someone who never stops talking, most people don't have the will to "jump right in."

I think she knew that, so she felt safe making the offer. My wife came up with the best rule for all us big talkers. If you're in a social setting, it should be equal. You shouldn't talk any more than another person. A simple idea. A *noble* idea. Easier said than done.

I understand people wishing each other happy holidays or Merry Christmas or Happy Hanukah. Whatever. But happy Ground Hog Day? That's what I heard on the radio recently on Ground Hog Day. I've always been more than a little bumped by Happy Memorial Day for obvious reasons. But I *really* can't wrap my brain around Happy Groundhog Day. Maybe the thing that bothers me the most about all these wishes for various happy days is people never seem to mean it anyway. Overwhelmingly people really don't care if you or I have a happy Groundhog Day. I feel like in general, if you don't mean it, don't say it. There would probably be a lot less talking but a higher percentage of sincerity.

Recently I was calling information to locate a certain CD I wanted. I called information several times for different store numbers, and each time a cheerful voice on a recording wished me a happy groundhog day – sometimes at the beginning *and* the end of the call.

No store had the CD I was looking for, so I was wished a happy groundhog day quite a few times. The combination of *no* store having the

CD, and the incessant wishes for me to have a happy groundhog day was starting to get to me. I mean who tells these people on these recordings to wish us a happy groundhog day and why? And does *anyone* working for the phone company seriously care if we have a Happy Groundhog Day? Phone company stop with the Happy Groundhog days – please! They won't stop.

I heard a good one the other day, while listening to a sports call-in show on the radio. The host took a guy's call, and the guy said "Hold on a minute," as though the host was at home and not on the air, where silence *isn't* golden. The host, of course, went to another call.

I can't seem to get over the degree of meanness all around us. From other countries towards us I get it, but here in America among ourselves every day, everywhere, it feels like shots, counter shots, zingers, and a whole lot worse.

You see it on television in debates. You endlessly read it in the newspapers – not *disagreement* – vicious attacks on character, intelligence – and worse. Several years ago,

Carol Burnett and I teamed up to promote the importance of friendliness. Phil Donahue gave us an hour, and we received 10,000 pieces of supportive mail. People wanted to join our organization, but we didn't have an organization. It was just our attempt at raising consciousness on the importance of friendliness. Not that I could have possibly expected it, but obviously it's had no effect at all.

I did hear that some local communities formed their own friendly groups. That was good. When Carol and I did this, it also generated some fun. David Letterman thought we were kidding. Merv Griffin gave us ninety minutes and had fun "You mean you're going to be friendly if a waiter spills soup on you?" Carol said "Yes," because he feels bad enough already."

James Wolcott in the Village Voice devoted a whole page to his outrage, that someone like me, who he said "Looks like he'd steal a tomato off your plate if you weren't looking" could possibly be espousing friendliness. They gave me a whole page to respond. I basically denied that I'd steal a tomato off your plate. So there were laughs and a lot of good feeling around this

twenty five years ago. Today, all this lack of
friendliness – grace – good will etc…I don't see
anything funny about it.

Because I'm involved with justice system issues,
I tend to joke around a lot in life for relief.
Believe me there's nothing even remotely
humorous about someone who shouldn't *be*
there spending their life in a cell, and I know the
cases, so I try to lighten my tension with humor.
It's not that unusual for my efforts at humor to
cause confusion.

The other day I phoned someone and his
assistant answered. I identified myself and the
lady said "Mr. Grodin, how *are* you?" I
kiddingly said "I'm sitting up. I'm taking
fluids." The woman said "Oh, have you been
ill?" "No, no, I said. I'm just joking." I then
went on to leave a message with the lady and at
the end of the call, she said "I hope you feel
better." I said Uh … uh …goodbye." I thought
of calling back, but it's a busy office, and I
figured I'd leave her alone.

I was talking to a young woman on the phone
the other day. She's an assistant in an office I

deal with. I should say, because it's relevant that it was an office that deals with show business. Well…actually every business has *something* to do with show business. At the end of what was a friendly business call, she said or I *think* she said "A big kiss." I told my wife this story; she said "You probably misheard her." She couldn't have said "A big kiss." I told this story to my daughter Marion who is in show business more than I am, and she said "A lot of people in show business end their calls by saying a big kiss." So now, I think I heard right. Oh well…the world won't come to an end over this.

I have a really bad habit. Sometimes when I'm talking to a woman – most often on the phone – I'll address them as "honey." This would be someone I know well or *not* that well. I wouldn't want someone to address my wife or daughter that way, unless they were really close, but I do it, even if I'm not close.

I'm doing it, because I want to communicate friendly feelings, but I really don't think it's a good idea. I thought about using "dear", but dear is about as offensive as honey. I've thought about using the woman's name more, but that *could* sound like I'm a teacher talking to a

student, so the "honey" keeps slipping out. I'm
sure it doesn't offend *every* woman, just some.
I'll keep working on it.

I'm banned from appearing in some places in my
area. I mean as a host or an M.C. for charitable
functions. Even though I do this for nothing,
I'm still banned. One group rightfully banned
me because in an attempt to be humorous, I said
introducing a very large local amateur singing
group "You don't have to audition to be in this
group, but that should in no way reflect on the
quality of the group." The audience laughed, but
the group didn't. It was a total joke.

In previous years I had heard them a couple of
times from back stage, and they sounded great.
Also at my final appearance for this organization
a couple of years ago – I kept needling the guy
referred to as the town troubadour, who was
known for his parodies he played on the piano. I
said things like "Imagine what it's like to live
with this guy?!

The audience laughed, and so did the
troubadour. I've run into the troubadour a few
times at the local market. It's all very friendly.

The other day I saw him there with his wife. I went over. We chatted a moment, and then I looked at his wife, and said "You look like you've really been through something living with this troubadour." She chuckled and said "It's been forty six years." Later I thought to myself she could have said "What's that supposed to mean?!" Humor is a dangerous business.

It's not easy to spot our flaws. It's human instinct to be on your own side. I mean if you're not on your side, *who's* going to be? In any case, I'm afraid I recently spotted a flaw I've had for many years. Just about every day I speak to a friend on the phone, and when I call and his secretary answers I say "Is he there?" Not, "Hi Pam, it's Chuck Grodin, how'ya doin?" Just "Is he there?"

It frankly hasn't occurred to me until recently that maybe *Pam* wants to chat. You need to know Pam is the secretary to my friend, who runs a network, so maybe, because she's got a lot of lines going, and "Is he there?" is o.k. On the *other* hand, years ago the wife of a close friend of mine complained about "Is he there?" She said "He?," like she was offended, I referred to her husband, whom I've known most of my life as *he*.

What really offended her was I wasn't chatting with *her*. *Her* husband wasn't running a network. He was just sitting around the house, and she wasn't answering a lot of phones, so "Is he there?" in that case was rude. So is it o.k. to say "Is he there?" or not o.k. to say "Is he there?"; that is the question.

Lately, I've been getting more and more invitations to events that have already taken place. I'm not really sure why that is. It *can't* be that they really don't want me there, but can say they invited me, if I run into them. Naah!

Besides these are big events not small dinner parties, so I could hardly cause any trouble at a *big* event – a small dinner party – maybe. I spoke to a friend of mine about this, and he said the same thing has been happening to him. He wondered, if you get an invitation to an event that's already taken place, do you still have to RSVP? No, I don't think we should take it personally. It's just a sign of our times where things don't quite work the way they used to.

I like reading advice columns. I find a lot of the questions and answers interesting. The other day a young woman who works for a large corporation wrote that she went to a formal luncheon, and she was very uncomfortable, because her supervisor had a disapproving look on her face every time their eyes met. The young woman felt maybe it had something to do with her table manners. She said she cut up the food on her plate into little pieces and then ate it, and she said when she finished, she put her napkin on her plate. She was asking the advice person if she had done something wrong?

The advice person said when you get up to leave, put your napkin on the *side* of the plate not on the plate. She said you should only cut one small piece of food at a time. She said only hold your utensils that you need when you are eating, and place them on the plate while you are chewing and talking.

I thought to myself "Hold it right there! Chewing and talking?" I thought chewing and talking was a major no no, and I'm not so sure you have to hold your utensils while you're eating either. I mean why?

The advice person also said when you finish
your meal place your knife and fork at 3 o'clock
on your plate. I guess the knife points to the 12
and the fork the three. I guess. I don't know –
the advice person's response made me really feel
sorry for the young woman. It also gave me a
slight headache. People who care so *much* about
this stuff should really make an effort to
consider more serious subjects. Like why are
you so *finicky*?! Finicky is defined as
excessively particular.

A recent study showed that men listen with half
of their brain and women listen with both sides.
People immediately thought that women are
better listeners. Not so fast! The professor who
did the study said it could mean that women find
the whole listening thing harder.

Just to further complicate it, he also said women
can handle listening to two conversations at
once. I knew a woman who acknowledged she
would consciously allocate a certain percentage
of her brain to listening while the rest of her
brain was off thinking about something else.
She also said "I'm sorry, what?" a lot.

I think you have to say the whole listening thing has a heck of a lot to do with circumstances. If you're a guy working in a field, alone from dawn to dusk, you come home, you're ready to listen to someone talk. If you're a woman working in a complaint department of a department store, you come home, and there are some complaints, which there always are, you'll go from listening on both sides of the brain, to listening on *no* sides of the brain.

My experience tells me that men generally listen better to other men and women to other women with the exception of first dates where everyone pays a kind of attention you seldom ever see again. Of course, the best way to get anybody to listen is to make the conversation about them, and *tell* them it is too. Just say "Listen to this story. You're in it."

If you would have told me I could lose my temper, because of one thing a total stranger said to me on the phone, I would say I'd be very surprised by that. Well, it recently happened, and I *was* very surprised. I was trying to contact someone I know at CNN to go on his radio show to promote a charity event. First they connected me to Atlanta for viewer's comments. I called back, and said I didn't want to comment.

I know the man, and I just want an office number. The woman said "I only have his cell phone number. Do you want that?" I said "No, I just want an office number." The woman again said "I only have his *cell* phone number. Do you want that?" I said "No. I just want an office number." She said in annoyance, "If you know him so well, why don't you want his cell?" I said "Oh, forget it!" and hung up. Of course, I never *said* I know him *so* well, and I felt it was too aggressive to call him on his cell. But my point is I don't know myself as well as I thought. Well…now I know myself a little better. The lesson? Everyone has a breaking point.

I pulled into a parking space outside some shops the other day, and a guy who was parked next to me backed out and crunched the right side of my car. He immediately took full responsibility – game me his name, phone number, etc.

But instead of this being a negative story, it turned out to be a wonderful story for me, because at the end of all the exchange of information, the fella looked at me and said

"Thanks for being so civil." The reason that meant so much to me is I've been asked more than a few times, if I ever get mad, and I always say I never do.

Well, as I've just said, I realize now I have gotten mad. I probably have crossed the line sometimes with *extremely* close loved ones, but *rarely*. I was happy to see, under duress which I'm under as much as your average person that I was who I claimed to be – someone who always respects the dignity of another person – no matter what. Of course, if someone hits my car again, well…we'll see what happens.

I'm usually not that interested in surveys, unless they confirm something *I've* been thinking. A new study by a research group called Public Agenda revealed that 79% of over 2,000 adults surveyed feel that a lack of respect and courtesy in American society is a serious problem. I couldn't agree more.

One of the biggest complaints is about customer service. I lost a credit card recently and was issued a new one. The instructions said I was to call an 800 number to get it activated. I was asked all kinds of questions to establish I was who I said I was. That was fine, but all through the call the woman was acting a little like a prosecuting attorney. I felt I was somehow being punished. "And what is your mother's maiden name?"

And of course one of everybody's favorites is being on hold for what feels like forever while a recording tells you how important your call is. Why are we becoming a rude society? One woman in Texas blamed Elvis. She said it started with Elvis shaking his hips. Hmmmm.

What's so bad about non sequiturs? I've been criticized more than a few times over the years for my non sequiturs. Someone in a group will be telling a story about a trip somewhere. The story ends. There's a decent enough pause, and I might tell a story about say a sporting event. Often someone will say "What's that have to do with the trip story?" In other words I'm chastised for my non sequitur. The dictionary defines non sequitur as "It does not follow."

So my sporting event story does not follow someone's story about a trip somewhere. Sue me! What's the big deal? I'm not putting down the trip story. I've just got a sporting event story. So? A friend I consulted on this said non sequiturs suggest a lack of interest in the previous subject. I admit I must not be interested enough in the story about a trip somewhere to come up with a travel story or at *least* some questions about the trip. Instead I go to my non sequitur sporting event story, and *maybe* it hurts the person's feelings, who told the travel story, and people notice. I say if you listen and show interest in the travel story, you can go to your sporting event story. I also say "Lighten up." Non sequiturs have gotten a bad rap.

I went over to get some work done on my car the other day. They told me it would take about a half an hour, so I went to read the paper in the little waiting area. There was a woman customer sitting there, and she was on her cell phone. "No!" she said in a voice you might use, if you're alone in a big house. "If I'm going to be late for work by five minutes, I don't bother to call, because I'll be there before you know it. Uh huh. Uh huh. Yeah! I don't like him either. No, he's a real jerk."

And on and on, and when she finished that call, it only took her a minute, before she was on to the next. "Hi! It's me!" I considered my options. I thought about taking out my own phone and launching into a fake conversation. Give her a taste of her own medicine. "Hey! How ya doin?! I'm in the waiting room while they're working on my car. It's the thermostat that controls how the heater works. Yeah. It's not working the way it should, so you don't get the right amount of heat, and it hurts your fuel efficiency. Uh huh. Uh huh." What is it with these people who talk on the phone as though they're alone – when they're in a public place?

If they *have* to be on the phone in public, they don't seem to even consider trying it this way. "Hi! I'm on a train, so I can't really talk, just make sure I didn't leave the oven on." But no! More likely it's "So what else?" The only solace I take from all of this is at least at some point I get off the train, and don't have to live with them.

I was invited to a party by a couple I met a few years ago. It was one of these "save the date" deals where they let you know about eight months ahead of time they're *having* a party. I like these people. They've got a dance floor that slides back and turns into a swimming pool, like

in the movie, *It's a Wonderful Life*. Months
after saving the date, I got another invitation that
said "The secret is out. It's black tie and wear a
crazy chapeau."

I'm assuming that this was a secret, because if I,
and I bet some others who saved the date knew
about the black tie and crazy chapeau thing, we
might not have saved the darn date in the first
place.

Unless it's part of my job, like most everyone, I
hate taking orders, and the black tie crazy
chapeau thing felt like an order to me. I
expected that in the military, where my wool
uniform really itched, but hey, it was the
military! Much earlier in grammar school, it
was single file, no talking, not one of my
favorites, but it was *school!*

But once you're out of school and the military, I
don't know about you, but I'm not crazy about
saving some date for a black tie and a crazy
chapeau. I got an idea since this couple seemed
to have an adventurous spirit, maybe they'd be
o.k. if I showed up with no tuxedo, just a regular
jacket with a black tie and a New York Met cap.

Since the Mets had a bad season, that certainly might qualify as a crazy chapeau. Or maybe I'll just go with the flow and do what they ask. I can tell you this though, the next time I'm saving some date, I want *all* the particulars.

I went to a restaurant the other day by myself. I sat down at a table, and it was freezing. The waiter came over, and I asked him to please make it less cold. Then I asked for some hot tea and a blanket. A man sitting alone nearby looked over at me and said "Thank you. It *is* freezing here."

A couple at another table said the same thing. Almost right away the temperature rose to a normal level, and everyone was happier. I've been told that the reason most people don't speak up about *anything* ridiculous that's happening is they're *shy*. When something is *obviously* wrong – don't be shy. Speak up – *politely* but speak *up*!

Not to be super picky, but there are three expressions that bump me. The least offensive, and many would say this isn't *remotely* offensive is when I say thank you to someone mostly at

stores, and the answer is often "No problem."
What happened to "You're welcome?" No
problem? How could there *possibly* be a
problem when someone hands me something I
bought and I say thank you? "No problem?" No
big deal? O.k. I'll give you that one. But I
really don't like it when someone says "You got
that right.", as though they are the ultimate
arbiter on *what's* right. My *least* favorite, and
thankfully I only know *one* person who says this
in response to something is, "*Exactly*." That one
really gets me. You think I'm being too picky?
You got *that* right.

Whether we like to admit it or not, we all have
downsides. The problem is we may be the last
person capable of *seeing* our downsides. Of
course, some people's downsides are a lot worse
than others. Downsides of *others* that bother me
are people who don't do what they say they're
going to do, people who are late, or early.

I'm not talking here about the kind of downside
that's *so* down it goes below a downside, like
lying, or cheating on your partner. That's *way*
lower than down. One of my least favorite
downsides comes from people, who seem to
constantly have a need to put others down – like

they don't have a downside. If you can change your downside people will enjoy your *upside* more. And if you can't spot your downside, ask a trusted friend, they'll tell you, and if they tell you that you don't *have* one – ask another friend.

I had an unusual experience recently. I was asked to speak at one of the stock exchanges in New York City. Y'know these are places filled with people buying and selling and *shouting* to each other over rows of people working their computers.

A highly unlikely place to speak, but there I was with others speaking on behalf of Mentoring U.S.A., a nonprofit organization that connects mentors to kids, who desperately need them. The only thing that could possibly quiet the group would be Let Us Pray, which I am not ordained in any way to say, so I spoke – *briefly*.

I saw a bumper sticker on the car in front of me that had parents bragging about their kid being an honor student. I felt bragging about *anything* in public was probably not a good idea. The next week I saw a bumper sticker that said "My kid beat up your honor student."

Most likely that was just a bumper sticker and not an actual report, but again public bragging at its best is offensive, and at its worst can be harmful to the health of you and your loved ones. The one exception to all of this, of course, is if you're running for office. Then I guess you have to brag and not worry about it, since probably about half the population hates you anyway.

What is it with these people, who feel compelled to tell you *every single thing* that's happened to them, since you last saw them? If you talked to them every day, it would be like – without you asking – "I had a pretty bad night's sleep. I feel a little better I had something to eat. I may go out later. I may not," and on and on.

Compelled. Compelled to tell. Can they help it? Probably not. Should we say something? If you can – preferably with humor. Will it work? Probably not. People who tell you *way* more than you can possibly be interested in are a different kind of bully. Look at yourself. Are you like that at all? If so, cut it out!

A woman wrote to an advice columnist recently complaining that though she sends cards noting people's birthdays, she seldom if ever gets a thanks or a card in return. She said she also sends cards for Easter, Thanksgiving, and even Halloween – a happy Halloween card?! But she *never* gets thanks or return cards on *those*. Eventually she stopped sending all these cards to all these people. No one complained about not getting them, so she couldn't feel hurt about not receiving thanks or a return card.

A good move on her part. What she didn't say in her letter was whether she had a job. I mean who has time to send happy Halloween cards to all your friends? Well, at least she's writing to the columnist – who *did* answer her, and basically congratulated her on finding a more comfortable way to live. I second that emotion. I find sending endless cards for whatever occasions and pouting, because you didn't get a return is really *reaching* for ways to feel bad.

Maybe what's bothered me the *most* about dentists is they don't seem to think there's anything odd about having a conversation with someone who can't answer them, because there's something in their mouths. *Mmm* seems to be a satisfactory response for them. My annoyance with this has gone to a new level in recent years.

Now the dentist seems to enjoy hitting me with what I'd say are some controversial opinions, and I'm still stuck with *mmm* as a response, when I promise you I've got a lot more to say than mmm. I think *dentists* more than most people enjoy having the last word.

Sometimes when I'm out with my wife and another couple for dinner, as everyone looks at the menu *I'll* order first, because I *know* what I'll order at least a day ahead of time. One or more people at the table will look at me as though I'm being rude – *ladies* order first! *I* order first to give everyone more time to study the menu – those who don't think ahead, as I do.

By trying to be considerate, I'm considered *rude*! It's as though I hope to *eat* before the others. First of all, as I've said, I almost *never* eat at dinner. I take home my order. I don't get out that much, and I have a lot to say – *eating* I can do alone. When I walk into a crowded restaurant with my wife – I go first and my wife says "Let me go first." Again, the implication is *ladies* go first. *I* go first to clear the way. No matter how hard you try to be *all you can be*, some people will take it the wrong way. It's called *life*.

CLOTHES

"With all due respect, count me out."

I bought a very expensive shirt the other day.

I was on my way to buy some more socks, when I spotted it hanging kind of alone. It's a long shirt jacket you don't tuck in, a color between charcoal gray and black. It's really good-looking. One of the many little cards hanging from it said it was 100% silk herringbone, imported fabric. Silk, herringbone, imported and fabric were all in capital letters. The shirt came with its own tiny little booklet.

First the booklet congratulated me on *buying* the shirt. It said the shirt "represented the finest in fabrics, craftsmanship and styling." It said the family that designed the shirt was "dedicated to upholding a 50 year tradition of excellence." It said they were "committed to providing sophisticated timeless fashions with unparalleled fit and attention to detail."

It said that their "uncompromising standards are evident in each piece of luxury clothing," and then on another little card that was attached by a string but not part of the booklet, it said "slubs and misweaves which appear in this fabric are not considered imperfections. They are inherent properties of this cloth and contribute to its uniqueness and natural beauty." I looked up "slub" in the dictionary, but it wasn't there, so that could be another imperfection from the shirt people.

Then I thought about the slubs and misweaves that might be in my expensive shirt. I tried to embrace the idea that they contribute to my shirt's uniqueness, kind of what you might see in an antique table or something, but this wasn't an antique table, it was a shirt that cost me a fortune. I've only worn the shirt once, and before I put it on, I hadn't read the literature on it, so I wasn't looking for any slubs and misweaves, and I've decided I'm not going to *start* looking for them either. All I know is the next time I do something that people find fault with, I'm going to say it's just part of my uniqueness. I recommend that for all of us.

For some reason I used to belong to a golf club, even though I don't golf. The *truth* is – it's a golf club, and I don't golf – *and* it turns out I go there about twice a year for lunch which considering the dues, costs me several thousand dollars for each lunch. These aren't *banquets*

[85]

I'm throwing. I go there with one other person.
I really didn't resign, because of the denim, but
on the other hand, what's the rap against *denim*?
I once saw a sign there that said Proper Attire
Required on Golf Course Please. I would have
no idea what proper attire for a golf course is,
jeans, a tuxedo – *what*?   Maybe we spend so
much time looking at clothes, because it's easier
to see that, than who's actually in them.

When I *would* go there occasionally for lunch,
they looked me over, as though it was
Buckingham Palace.   I mean guys we're sitting
around in *shorts*. At one point I was stopped by
a man and a woman, as I entered the dining area.
I thought it was because I was wearing a cap, but
no, it wasn't my cap – it was my denim shirt –
no *denim* allowed.

I have since learned they *could* have gotten me
on two counts – the denim and the fact that the
denim wasn't tucked *in*. I guess they figured,
since I readily agreed to give up the denim shirt
for a cotton shirt they *gave* me to *keep* – why
even mention the not tucked in issue?   I
eventually resigned from the club. I'm positive
they're going to think it's because of the whole
denim thing, which it absolutely *isn't*.

[86]

I bought a cotton flannel shirt the other day, and took a look at the instructions of how to wash or clean it. I was really surprised that the label said "Flammable should not be worn near sources of fire." What?! Does that mean I better take this shirt off, before I make a cup of coffee? What if I'm somewhere, where there's a fireplace? If I'm wearing my new shirt, should I immediately leave the room? I'm adding this to my long list of things I don't really understand.

You gotta be "in." I went to a store the other day to buy a pair of pants. I saw a pair I liked, but the salesman, whom I knew refused to sell them to me. He said he still hadn't gotten over seeing me wear cashmere on television in the Summer time.

"People must have thought you were in reruns!" he said, barely able to contain his agitation, so he absolutely refused to sell me these pants because they weren't...I forget what. Actually I came back about an hour later, looked around, didn't see him and bought the pants. He spotted me, as I was leaving. I apologized, and he was pretty nice about it, but he didn't completely conceal his disdain.

I mean they were *selling* them there! I pay the price for not being *in* with the snickers and smirks I get from the people, who really know 'what's the latest.' It all reminds me of a segment of Candid Camera from years ago.

Five people were in the waiting room of a doctor's office. Everybody was with Candid Camera but one guy. The Candid Camera people all stood. The guy looked around seemed puzzled but stood. They sat. He sat. They stood again and he stood, and then they sat, and he sat as though nothing unusual had happened. It's called "Going with the flow." Not for me and a lot of the rest of us.

I was in Florida recently, and I ran into a curious dress code issue. A group of us, some wearing *caps* went to a restaurant. There were many people there wearing *shorts*, but after we were sitting at our table for about ten minutes the maitre d' came over and *very* nicely said "Can I impose on you to take off your caps."

We nodded to him, and as he walked away our group decided to find another place. One of my friends said to the maitre d' as we were leaving "We don't want to make you uncomfortable, and we don't want to be uncomfortable." We all had long pants on too! Actually neither caps nor shorts bother me. My problem is loud music. It's just another item for us humans to disagree on.

My feet get cold in the wintertime. Actually they're cold all year round, so socks take on a greater importance for me than for your average person. I've had a lot of problems with socks. For years even though they were the right size, I had to tug and pull to get certain socks on. Socks have caused me back problems.

A couple of years ago I was in this very upscale store looking for some socks that would keep my feet warm and not throw my back out. I came across some eighty percent cashmere socks that promised to be as warm as toast and go on like butter. They cost forty five dollars a pair. The ones that came higher up the leg were fifty. I bought so many I later heard the guy who sold them to the store had my picture up in his office. They were warm. They went on effortlessly.

They were wonderful, until around the third washing, when they began to fall apart. By the fifth washing I could see my toes and heel through the socks.

I took a pair back to the store. The clerk, not the one who sold them to me, I think he was hiding in the back, told me that "Cashmere doesn't wear well at all. In a short while it really starts to fall apart." I said "I know." It took about a year, but eventually I got a 50% refund.

I decided to drive to a less upscale area to see what people *there* paid for socks. I went into the first store I saw that sold socks and almost fainted when I saw I could get some pretty darned good looking socks for $3.99 on sale. I quickly snapped up a dozen. I came home. I put them on right away, no back strain. They were fabulous. Easy to get on – felt good. I haven't washed them yet, but they're not cashmere, so I'm pretty hopeful. I never imagined new socks could bring me this much happiness.

I went to a shoe store the other day, and the young woman who was waiting on me had several small earrings on her ears along with some large ones, as well as a small earring on her nose. She also had a large Band-Aid above her eye. I asked if she'd had an earring over her eye that had gotten infected? She said no. She had an earring there that the store felt was one earring too many, so she covered it with the Band-Aid during work hours. Your guess is as good as mine as to why management objected to the eye earring, and not the nose earring.

I had a fella who worked with me for about ten years, first as a driver and then as a producer who insisted on wearing sweats, pretty much at all times. He's a graduate of Yale, a really smart charming nice guy, who's more comfortable in sweats. Who isn't? The fact that everyone else at work was mostly in jackets and ties didn't trouble him at all, but of course, it troubled some of them.

If you do a good job, which he did, I'm not the kind of person who's going to tell you what to wear, so I withstood some pressure from management, and he stayed with his sweats. At some point, he probably sensed that while I wouldn't ask him, I could probably spend my time more fruitfully not fending off management on his sweats, so he went to jeans and a sweatshirt.

That lasted about two weeks, and then he said something about needing more pants room for a bad knee, and went back to sweats. The few times we did talk about it, he quite passionately said people should worry more about their values and the quality of their work than their clothes.

I had too much other stuff on my mind to make a case against him, and honestly who wants to argue with someone about what they wear? It's more than enough we do it with our kids, so if everyone wore sweats and earrings on their ears, eyes, nose and even mouth, would the world be a better or worse place? At those moments, when I'm forced to put on a tuxedo, I lean toward the earrings and sweats, well maybe not the earrings.

Where was the representative for us men when someone came up with the idea of neck ties? The words alone "*neck ties*" should have provoked an emergency meeting. I'm really not someone who likes to dress up and go out, and one of the reasons for this is "*neck* ties." If I buy a dress shirt, no matter how good quality it is, after a certain amount of launderings, buttoning the button at the neck is punishment, and I refuse to believe that it's because I may have gained a couple of pounds.

To avoid the problem I'd have to buy a shirt that's way too big – which, let's face it is not a million dollar look. There's no easy answer to this, but here's my hope. We've undergone many changes in America in my lifetime. I'm hopeful that someday neck ties are a thing of the past through *fashion* changes or even if necessary *legislation*.

Do you ever wear thermals, or what some people call long johns? I do, and I not only wear them in the wintertime, fall and spring as well, and on a cool summer night, they're not out of the question for me either. What really startles some people, who know me, is I wear them *indoors* as well. Maybe not indoors in the summer, but *possibly* then too. Also I'll probably be sorry I say this, but I almost never get sick. Friends who point fingers and ridicule me often have to stop pointing to sneeze or cough.

I've been told over and over that staying warm has nothing whatsoever to do with catching colds. Again I'm told this by people who catch a lot of colds. It's "germs in the air" they say. Nothing to do with staying warm.

Obviously I'm not a scientist or doctor, but I can tell you from keeping a pretty steady eye on this situation for years, that when you're even a little bit chilly those widely accepted "germs in the air" make their move, and I think this applies to people of all ages. Some have said to me "If you're wearing a pair of long johns indoors, in the summertime, what do you do outdoors in the winter time?"

First of all, you're not going to *see* me outdoors in the winter time all that often, and if I am, it's rarely long enough for any germs to spot me, but just in case I'm out there for say five minutes, I've gone to *two* pairs of long johns and even three, and while I'm at it I throw on a thermal shirt over an undershirt which is already under a flannel shirt, which is under a sweater, which is under a heavy jacket.

I know this sounds like I put an awful lot of thought into thermals, but I put almost no thought at all into colds. Now, of course, none of this applies if you can honestly say you don't ever feel chilly, and some people claim that's true, but I don't really believe it. I think it's a macho thing to say that. I think actually most people don't give much *thought* to any of this.

Years ago I spent some time outdoors in the wintertime watching my son play football. I'd be standing on the sidelines next to other dads, who'd be *freezing*. They'd say things like "Wow, it's freezing." I was perfectly fine. I'm not really comfortable sharing how many long john pants and thermal shirts I had on then. Suffice to say I looked like a former player.

For some time now, I've been looking for a special pair of sweat pants. Well…not sweat pants exactly, more like lounge pants. I'm a lot more interested in lounging than sweating. Something in a fleece – a soft material…for *lounging*! The stores have a lot of them, but they don't have flys – a zipper – buttons. Call me fancy. I'm a guy. I like a fly. I don't like the choices, if you *don't* have a fly. I've asked a number of sales people, why the lounge pants or the sweats don't have flys? No one seems to know.

After a couple of months of this, I decided to take the matter into my own hands. I headed out to two stores I hadn't been to. I just could not believe there were no soft fleece lounge pants with flys to be found. Just as in every other store, the salesperson said they had no such thing. This time I smiled, and said I'll just look around. It was a big store.

I perused every department that sold any kind of clothes for men and eventually off in a corner – soft fleece lounge pants with a fly! I went to another big store and had the exact same experience. There are two morals to this story – or lessons anyway.

To you men out there who *want* soft fleece lounge pants with a fly – they're out there – you just have to work at it a little to find them. The other lesson is to the store owners or managers. Get the salespeople to familiarize themselves more with what they've got to sell. It will be better for everyone.

I've always wondered why men didn't rise up against the concept of the tuxedo when it was initially thrust on us. Maybe in those days people were so buttoned up it never occurred to any man to say "Aw, no you don't!"

I would say the same when they came up with the whole *cuff link* thing and of course ties. Now we have a men's designer who's won the Council of Fashion Designers of America Award as men's wear designer of the year, who wears no socks and pants so short they show bare ankle and around three inches of shin. Give me a break!

Oh yeah, his suits on average cost thirty five hundred dollars! It's kind of a Pee Wee Herman look. Brooks Brothers has signed him to do a collection, and according to someone speaking on behalf of Bergdorf Goodman this designer, Thom Browne is a top selling line. By the way he spells Tom T H O M and Brown B R O W N E. Not to be super picky – but *c'mon!*

Evidently none of his customers wear their pants as short as he does, but I'm assuming some go for the no socks show ankle look. With all due respect – count me out. As I've said, I *like* socks, and I certainly have no intention whatsoever of showing shin.

I bought a sweater the other day and felt as though I had entered a whole new world. In reasonably small letters on the left front it says Paul and Shark. The salesman said it was an English company that was bought by an Italian company, or maybe it was the other way around. Paul and Shark I guess are two guys named Paul and Shark, although it's hard to imagine Shark was his given name.

The main reason the sweater took me into a whole new world was that it allows me to accumulate miles. I'm not sure what kind of miles. I don't think they're *flying* miles, because I couldn't spot anything about flying in all the literature that came with my sweater. What it actually said was "miles that will eventually let you have access to a lot of premiums."

It also said I could become a member of the Paul and Shark club. I guess if I really concentrated I could figure out what it all means, but I'm choosing to spend my mental energy elsewhere these days. When I buy a sweater, just give me the sweater. Cleaning instructions? Fine. But the rest of it? Let me out of here.

We're a nation filled with critics. Probably every country is, and sometimes it seems the critics run out of stuff to criticize. Recently I read a criticism of how the coach of the New England Patriots football team, Bill Belichick dresses on the sidelines during a game.

He wears sweats or something – sweat *pants* anyway. The writer criticizing the sweats prefers how the former coach of the Dallas Cowboys, Tom Landry dressed on the sidelines. He wore a suit and tie *and* a fedora. To me he looked like he was headed toward an important meeting, and just stopped on the way to coach the game.

TECHNOLOGY

"Let me out of here."

I have been having some very nice conversations lately with recordings. Most recently I had one with a recording for the phone company. I was calling to report static on my line. When I call a number other than local, I get a tremendous amount of static. It's not the most interesting subject in the world. If I told *you* all about it, believe me it wouldn't hold your attention, but the recording from the phone company seemed *incredibly* interested. It asked me every conceivable question about my static you could think of – and some you couldn't. It was a very nice experience. Having someone show that much interest in what you have to say is a very nice experience, even if it *is* a recording.

I always try as hard as I can not to be too demanding, so if I ask for something to be done – I ask myself is this request reasonable? This one is. I and I'm sure many of you when making a phone call often have to look at our phone book *while* making the call if it's not a familiar number. The phone company disconnects the call too soon, if there's a pause too long for them. Phone company, *please* don't do that. I know this is all automated. Re automate please. Even if re automate is not a word, please re automate.

A friend of mine was told he had a medical problem. Unlike me, he just took the doctor's diagnosis and plans to begin a complicated treatment.   On matters of degree of medical seriousness, I get *three* opinions. Without asking him, I decided to pursue another opinion for him. After a phone call I got a doctor's name to call to discuss my friend's problem.

He is with Cornell Weill Medical Center in New York. I called information to get their number. That's when the trouble started. I'd say to the recording Cornell etc. The recording would say Columbia etc. Three times I called information. I said *Cornell*. They say Columbia. I gave up on information and just got an operator at a local hospital on the phone. The connection wasn't clear. At some point I said – whatever, trying to corroborate what the operator had said. She responded with irritation "That's *not* what I said. That was just the *beginning* of this story. Nothing's easy.

There's a moment in the movie *For Your Consideration* where the *extraordinarily* gifted actress Catherine O'Hara, playing an acting teacher, watches a scene between a young man and woman. After the scene she goes to show the young actress how it should be done and plays her part. When she finishes, she says to the class "See the difference?"

The class looks puzzled, and then one young male student tentatively asks "It's *louder*?" There are so many people *everywhere* who speak with great authority, who absolutely don't know what they're talking about! My latest was a call to information 411, for a phone number, and the operator said to me "You can't get information from the phone you're using." I said "Oh, thank you," dialed 411 again and got the number. *Always* be respectful, but it's *often* a good idea to be skeptical.

I don't know how to work most things. I just don't. Sometimes I can't even get the television to go on. Recently a man came to where I live to fix a television set. He moved some wires around as I stared. Then he asked me "Where's your modem?" Well, I'm betting not *everyone* who's reading this knows what a modem is.

I don't. I called my wife, and she told me. Recently, another guy came to fix some power outage. After watching him go down to the basement and back up three times, I *thought* he said "I have to go to the bathroom." I asked "You have to go to the bathroom?" He said "No. I said I'm baffled." So *he* was baffled too. Whatever your problem is, take some solace in that you're not alone.

I got this little CD player with a head set. People really recommended it for relaxation. I said "Relaxation?" – so I got it. My wife helped me to understand how to work it. It was great the first few times. Then my weaknesses took over. I can turn a light switch on and off, but I've never had a typewriter, a computer – no e-mail, so of course eventually I wasn't able to operate the CD player.

The word "error" kept coming up on the screen which gave me a chest pain. In other words, when you're stressed think of something *fun* to do – even eating a donut would qualify.

It's struck me lately that I have an awful lot of conversations these days with recordings. The *down* side is I'm talking to *recordings,* and I really don't understand *how* I can be talking to *recordings* – going back and forth with question and *answers.* On the other hand there's never really a chance for – a disagreement over *something* – nice.

I called information the other day, and the recording said something I've never heard before "The number you have reached has been reported to be in trouble." Numbers can have *difficulty* on the line, but trouble? Here's trouble. You're seriously ill, and you're an atheist. You can't get along with your partner *and* several others.

You find yourself under enormous stress just carrying out your normal job. Those are just a *few* examples of trouble. Telephone numbers can only have *difficulty* on the line. To have trouble you have to be alive – human – animal – insect – whatever. If you're *alive*? There's among *other* things – trouble.

When I was a boy attempting to grow up, we had no cell phones, iPhones, iPads and *endless* amount of other technology that is now available – *none* of which as I've said, I've chosen to have. There's been much said about all of this, but I heard the most salient point recently. "Technology is far exceeding content." O.k. I'm going to take a walk now – then take a shower.

If I ever needed any proof, which I don't that I come from a different world technologically speaking anyway, I got it from a recent piece in the New York Times business section. I read it, because the headline had the words pen and paper. Remember those? The full headline was a "Tool for Tablet Users Who *Crave* Pen and Paper."

Here's the first paragraph of the article. "Seeking to cater to fans of ink and paper, Livescribe has created the Sky smartpen, a writing tool with a tiny computer inside that records notes written on microdot paper. The notes are then sent wirelessly to a personal account in the *cloud* through a partnership with Evernote, the digital archive service." There was much more, but *let me out of here!*

This comes under the heading of "Just when I thought I'd heard everything. We're *used* to getting calls from those 800 numbers conducting surveys, but recently I got a call – the screen said 800 etc. I answered it – intending to ask the person to take my number off the list. Instead I heard a *recording* saying "All of our representatives are busy with other calls. Please hold and someone will be with you shortly." I mean they called *me*! Oh yeah, I hung up, and thankfully they haven't called back – yet.

Breakdowns in efficiency are not exactly a breaking news story these days. Stores don't open when the sign on their door says they're supposed to. I went into a market one morning recently – bought some food and there was no way to pay for it.

None of their cash registers were open. A clerk stared at me for a second and said "You come in her all the time – pay for it next time." *I* did, but *c'mon...*

More recently I called a friend of mine at the New York Times – a recording said his mailbox for messages was full so the recording transferred me to another recording that transferred me back to my friend's full mailbox, and the recording again said it would transfer me to .....The New York Times?! Fellas, c'mon...

I had to put my car in the shop recently, so the dealership gave me a loaner – a 2012, model of my 2004 car. The technology had *advanced* to such a degree I needed to have the dealer show me how to turn on the engine. As he sat there in the car with me I asked him how to turn on the lights, the radio and about a half dozen other things that just had symbols. Finally he admitted *he* was confused.

When the technology gets so *advanced* that the dealer can't even follow it – what *is* the point *really*? I was with a record company executive the other day. He told me CD's, DVD's and about a half dozen other things we know are soon to be extinct. Manufacturers should understand that newer is not necessarily better.

We got a new television set recently with all the advanced technology. Here's what it says on the remote control. Muting, t.v. video, power, t.v. power, DVR, DVR/VCR, SAT/Cable, t.v., jump out, MTS, SAP, Freeze, Sound, Picture, T.V./SAT, wide, guide, SVR display, wega/gate, tools, prev replay, advance, next visual search, pause, stop, Vol., Ch. After pressing a number of buttons, I was able to get *half* of a picture on one channel. It was a man on stage lecturing about how important it is to love. Well…I'm all for love, but at *that* moment – it wasn't coming easily.

I was a co-host of a charity event in my area last week, and the people in charge of the event gave me a beautiful clock, as a gesture of their appreciation of my showing up. It's a *really* beautiful clock, but when you look at it, there's no way you can actually tell what time it is. I'm looking at it now. It doesn't have numbers. I think they're Roman numerals, but the numbers are so small it's hard to tell. I'm really not sure what to do with it. I don't mean to sound ungrateful, but do *you* want a clock sitting there, where you can't tell the time?

What happened to rakes? Oh, I know they're still around, but mostly I'm hearing leaf blowers, as loud a noise pollution that we have. I realized they're more efficient that rakes, and I know they're here to stay, but I wish we could have had a vote on it.

I played a veterinarian once in a movie who gave a horse too much anesthesia on the operating table, and the horse died. When the owner showed up to see how the horse was doing, I said "I'm sorry, we lost him." The owner indignantly shouted, "You lost him?! How could you lose him? Don't you have people who *watch* the animals?"

I was thinking about this when I heard we either lost some nuclear secrets or had them stolen or something. Don't we have people who watch the nuclear secrets? I don't know when I've ever had anything to do with the government, I feel like I've had to fill out a ton of forms, before anyone will even talk to me. Steal nuclear secrets?! It boggles the mind.

It's got to be the new technology. Download and hard drive and all that. I recently had a book I wrote handed to me on something smaller and thinner than a playing card. I guess our nuclear secrets can easily go on something like that. In the old days they probably were on a lot of papers or something a lot bigger than a playing card. Sometimes bulk is good. Harder to steal. The world is really getting complicated. It feels like now we have to have people watching the people, who watch the people. On the other hand if someone stole our secrets, then we probably can steal *their* secrets. It's a heck of a way to go through life.

I was startled the other day to see a correspondent on CNN coming out against *fax* machines. He was *sincerely* making *fun* of people with fax machines. My fax machine is my *only* bow to modern technology.

I sometimes *watch* my assistant in her office watching her computer to I *guess* come *up* after it's gone *down,* or maybe it has a *fever*?! I don't even want to *ask* what that little dot or arrow *is* that keeps moving around. So *please* (you on CNN) don't make fun of my fax machine. Oh, it's not perfect – it will beep and clank from time to time for no discernable reason – to *me* anyway. Sometimes it buzzes that a fax is coming through that never does – but it *never* goes down or has a fever. Respect is due for my fax machine – please!

I make an unusual effort *I* think, to always at least *try* to be nice to everyone – no matter what. I'm really put to the test when I regularly get calls mostly from earnest young *women* trying to make a living telling me I can now have their high speed internet *something*. I tell them I won't even be able to follow what they're saying.

I tell them I'm a writer, and the first thing I wrote was produced in New York in the 60's, and I've never had a *typewriter*. It doesn't stop them. They plow ahead telling me something about a cell phone I could have with 200 free minutes. They continue to plow ahead. "Thank you. Thank you." I say "Thanks a lot." Thanks for everything. Eventually the call mercifully comes to an end. I think I'm living in the wrong century.

That I don't have a computer really seems to upset more than one person in my life. "You don't have a computer!? How could you not have a computer!? You don't e-mail!? How could you not *e-mail*!?" I have *written* lots of stuff in my life. Books, movies, plays, t.v. specials, thousands of commentaries, and *I don't have a computer*. If you want to e-mail me to let me know what you think of what I've written – you *can't*! You can e-mail my assistant, but not me, and she *only* shows me what she thinks I need to see. You'd have to write me or phone me (I have caller I.D.) – *or* fax me.

I *do* have a fax machine, however there's not a heck of a lot of people, who have my fax machine number. I *don't* have a typewriter. Do they still make them? The fax machine malfunctions so much, I'm thinking of *not having* a fax machine. *I'm* thinking of it.

I'll probably just get a new one. Have you ever bought a new fax machine – got the cartridges in place and made sure everything was connected right? I have. I'd rather have a bad cold.

There's a lovely fella at my house a lot who deals with the problems of my wife and son's computers. I also see him a lot over at a buddy's house working on his computer. Again, a lovely guy, but I *have* enough family members and close friends. No, the state of trying to get something to work or waiting for something to be fixed is not a state I want to live in or even visit. I guess it could change, but as they say in politics, at this point in time, that's why I don't have a computer.

I'm one of these people who goes to the *full* service pump at the gas station. No self-service for me! I realize that might make me sound self-indulgent or lazy, but I'm really not. I guess I could figure out the whole self-service thing, but I've tried it a couple of times, and the rules seem to vary at the different gas stations. Not only that, but I'm not *entirely* confident I won't spill some gasoline on my pants.

My problem is the full service opportunities seem to be diminishing. I've passed more than a couple of my old full service places that are now only *self*-serve, so sometimes I have no choice but to go to the self-service pump. I approach it with trepidation. I took a test once when I was around fifteen that indicated I was in the lowest twelfth of the nation in electrical and mechanical aptitude. That's my explanation for going for full service.

I know couples, and I'm sure some of you do too, who have recordings of themselves singing when their answering machine picks up. Am I being too critical, or doesn't that seem more than a little narcissistic? I'm calling to talk to someone or leave a message – not to hear someone sing.

I've got plenty of C.D.'s of my favorite singers. I just have no interest in hearing someone sing when I call them, unless maybe it's Neil Diamond, whom I've never called. I don't get it, or maybe I do.   Answering machines are for leaving messages. If you want to sing, try out for a musical.

Do you have a great need when you phone someone or someone phones you to *see* the other person? That's what a videophone can do for you. A picture-phone was demonstrated over forty years ago at the New York World's Fair, and there wasn't exactly a stampede to get one. There *still* isn't.

Of course, they've improved on the technology over the years, so the video quality is better. Still I don't sense a run on them. Do you want to spend any time on your appearance, before you make or receive a phone call? I didn't *think* so. Technology is always coming up with new things – because they *can*. And we often don't rush out to buy them, because – we don't *want* to.

I went to radio shack the other day to buy a radio, but Radio Shack was *out of radios*! Y'know; the big rush during the holiday season. Oh, they *had* radios but with short wave, which I'm not looking to get. It reminds me too much of World War II. They *did* have *weather* radios and CB and Ham radios, scanners and multi band radios, business and marine radios.

They had the Grundy G5 AM/FM/SW radio. They had they Grundy 5350 Deluxe AM/FM/SW radio. They even had the Eton American Red Cross FR300 multi-purpose radio model NG5350DLB radio that blends the best of yesterday and today. They had an AM/FM radio that has TV-VHF flashlight siren and wireless phone charger – and NOAA – *whatever* that is and many more exotic things. Suffice to say, they didn't have just an AM/FM radio. Just a little plain radio – they didn't have.

Can you understand what it says on your car's dashboard? I have no idea what RND or ASL mean. I guess if I studied my booklet it's in there, but I hate studying the booklets. I guess I could also understand how to use the memory aspect on the radio as well – *if* I studied my booklet.

I could also possibly get on top of seek and scan, *if* I studied my booklet. Maybe I'm not remembering it right, but in the old days you didn't have to study a booklet so much if at *all*. You turned the radio on. You tuned to the station – that's it. I know a lot of people really appreciate all this high tech stuff, but I'm not one of them, and I get the feeling I'm not alone.

More and more machines are taking over. I went to a market the other day and when I got to the checkout counter, there was no clerk – just a thing of some kind where you were supposed to press all kinds of buttons. I had no idea what was expected of me.

Luckily a roving clerk came over and did it for me. I'd like to think I wasn't the only customer who needed help. A couple of days later the same thing happened in a parking garage. Again, no clerk – just a machine to punch. Again I was lost. Again a roving clerk came to my rescue. He explained it's a way garages save money. I'm happy for the stores and garages, but let me out of here. More *people*. Less machines!

This comes in the just when I thought I heard everything department which is getting to be a bigger and bigger department. Someone has come up with a concept of how Mona Lisa would sound, if we could have heard her speak. Somebody measured something with computers, of course, the width of her mouth, cheekbones, who knows what else, and suddenly I'm listening on the radio to Mona Lisa talking.

I was so struck by the weirdness of the concept I can't even tell you what language she was speaking. It may even have been English. Who are we going to hear next Washington, Lincoln? Next we'll hear the computer generated voice of George Washington endorsing Cheerios. I wish I was kidding. There ought to be a law, and I don't believe there is one.

When I got on that Do Not Call list that was put into effect years ago, the number of calls I got from people selling things at all hours of the day has pretty much disappeared. Now they're faxing! They're faxing me offers of vacations, cruises, etc., etc., etc., at all hours!

But recently I noticed at the bottom of these faxes there's a number to call to get on the Do Not *Fax* list, so I called it, and I'm on *that* Do Not List, except a couple of numbers when I call, they say this is not a *working* number, and you wonder why *bars* do well.

In the long list of things I don't really understand is my interaction with the telephone company's information service – 411. I dial 411 for a number. A recording asks for city and state. I give it. The recording repeats it and says "Is that right?" I say "yes." The recording then asks me to say the listing I want.

I say something like "Acme Hardware." The recording says "Acme Hardware. Is that right?" I say "Yes." The recording then says "Hold for a specialist." Hold for a specialist?! I thought the recording and I were getting along great, and then the recording bumps me over to a specialist. Don't get me wrong. The specialists are nice too. I just don't understand the problem between me and the recording.

I have a close friend who always answers his cell phone no matter what he's doing. I mean he could be an EMS worker in the Hudson River rescuing people from Captain Sully's plane, and he'd answer and say "Let me call you back, I'm just rescuing people in the Hudson River." All phones and cell phones should have caller I.D. so you can choose to only answer if it's your spouse or children. Even then my friend would answer and explain he's in the water rescuing people.

I got a new cell phone recently. The guy at the cell phone store laughed when he checked his computer and learned how old my *old* cell phone was. I'm not saying he laughed at *me*, but he laughed. It wasn't a little laughter either.

I've really been focusing on how to master my new cell phone. The only reason I *have* a new cell phone is I lost my old cell phone. That's a whole other story. Anyway I've really been making an uncharacteristic effort to master my new cell phone – y'know like how to turn it on and off. The other day with my wife standing by (she went to Dartmouth) I turned my phone on, and it said I had a message.

I've *never* been able to retrieve a message from a cell phone, and even though I carefully followed instructions – I still couldn't retrieve it. My wife said she felt with a proper effort on my part I could eventually retrieve a message. She said "I don't see you on a computer," but I do think you could retrieve a message on your cell phone – *some*day. One of the many reasons I love my wife is she doesn't have unrealistic expectations of me.

Everyone tells if I had me if I had a computer I could easily access information, but I feel like from *non* computer sources I'm *already* on information overload. Then there's the e-mail you can do with a computer. People are polite to me when they hear I don't have e-mail. *Shocked* but polite. Frankly as time goes by, I'm trying to be in touch with *less* people not more.

I was at a friend's house the other day and he was sending out some e-mails. I asked "If you don't get a response to your e-mail, is that like not having a phone call returned?" "A little," he grudgingly admitted. Who needs that feeling?

So all in all not having a computer is fine with me. I am happy for all of you who are happy to have your computers. I really am. From what I've experienced and observed, sustained happiness is one of life's hardest goals to attain, so if your computer helps you get there – and it does for the people in my own family – then good for you.

I recently had a very pleasant experience talking to a lady from Delta airlines. She was a recording, but it was actually a better experience in some ways than you can have talking to a person. First she *very* cheerfully said "Hi." Then she said at any point I could simply say "Help." She also said she didn't mind interruptions. Where are you going to find an actual person like that? She was *special*.

TRAVEL

"I really don't want to do this."

I believe this is a good example of less is more, or less is *enough*! Recently I was on the phone with someone making an appointment. She gave me the street and the address. I said "Okay. Good. I know where that is." She then said "You go past the Baskin Robbins, the Mobil Station, and Radio Shack. If you reach Wal Mart, you've gone too far." Throughout all this – I'm saying "Okay. Fine. Got it. Yes. I know where you are." She continued "It's right across the street from the big rug store." Sometimes less is *really* better.

All the recent talk about sleepovers at the White House got me to thinking about when I visited there during the Reagan years. I was friends with a fellow close to the administration, and he took me around and introduced me to different people.

One of them walked me outside on the grounds late at night and pointed up at President Reagan's bedroom window. There was a big tax cut he was supposed to announce the next day, that a lot of people felt was bad for the deficit, and I was thinking about tossing a pebble at his window, and asking him not to announce it. I was envisioning the President in his pajamas opening the window and saying, "What is it?"

Soon a Secret Service agent appeared and very nicely suggested we stroll elsewhere. Nobody asked me to sleepover, and if they had, I wouldn't have done it. For me sleepovers are too much trouble. First of all, even at the White House, I would ask if the blankets were freshly cleaned. They usually *aren't* anywhere. Then I'd want to be able to have a latch on the door, so you can lock it from inside for every reason you can think of.

I always ask for that, and often the hotel manager says "Only hotel personnel have keys to the rooms," as though that's supposed to be of great comfort to me. I'm sure they don't have any latches that work only from the inside at the White House. They wouldn't want some foreign dignitary, who didn't get what he wanted to lock himself in his room.

And definitely even the White House isn't going to be prepared for my mattress requirement. Other than home, no mattress I visit is hard enough for me, so I need a board not underneath the mattress. That really doesn't work for me but on *top* of the mattress covered with a lot of blankets, so it's not *too* hard. I've figured this out through trial and error. Then you put your sheet over it and make the bed, with those fresh blankets. Now President Reagan always seemed like a pretty easy going guy, but even *he* wouldn't have wanted *me* for a sleepover.

I wouldn't wish that everyone be like me, because the economy might come to a total stand still. As I've said, I *really* don't like to travel. When I hear about these long delays at airports – flights cancelled, terminals closed. When I hear an hour more or less to get out of New York to go over the George Washington bridge to get in our out of the Lincoln or Holland tunnel... Bless you who do it, but count me out. A few weeks ago someone at the market asked me if I'd be traveling this summer? I said "I may go downstairs." I really admire all you people who went away for the holidays. *I* stayed home.

I pretty much always like to stay home – *on* the holidays and *not* on the holidays. But you people who leave home and go somewhere I really admire. My friend Henry Schleiff who I feel is the single funniest person I've ever met called me over the holidays from Nieves. I'm not sure where that is, but Henry was down there with his wife Peggy and their sons Harry and Sidney.

Henry said they're all having a great time, but it took forever and ever and *ever* to get there. Flight delays. Cancellations. Lost luggage. Forever. Henry said he thought it took around the same amount of time to get to Nieves, as it would to get to the moon. So I'm sitting here at *home* in admiration of all you people who keep *leaving* home and going to all these faraway places – even if "In the same amount of time you could go to the moon."

Unlike some of my closest friends and family, food is the last thing I'm interested in when choosing a restaurant. Don't get me wrong, of course, I like food, but unlike others of more discerning taste, I just about always find the food served *wherever* I go up to my standards. O.K. no cracks about my standards. The most important consideration for *me* in choosing a restaurant is not food, but how *far* it is from where I live.

For some time now, when I do go out because of the influence of family and friends I find myself driving around twenty five minutes each way to the restaurant. The place I generally go to by everyone's account has great food, and because of that it's always packed, and because of *that* it's so noisy you can barely hear what anyone is saying – which happens to be my *second* most important requirement in choosing a restaurant.

Close to home is first. *Hearing* people is second. What I eat comes third. Unfortunately in my group I'm in a minority of one, so for everyone to get the best food I continue to drive to restaurants that are far away where I can barely hear anything, and the food tastes pretty much the same to me as closer quieter places.

There are some things, if I lived forever, I will never understand. A report from the Reuter's news agency tells us a German travel agency is offering special flights for people who prefer to fly nude. You must enter and exit the plane fully clothed but *in* flight – you can be nude.

The crew will remain clothed throughout the flight for safety reasons – whatever that means. So the captain and co-pilot *won't* be nude.

Good! A spokesman for the airline said "I don't want people to get the wrong idea. It's not that we're starting a swinger club in midair. We're a perfectly normal holiday company." Well....I guess it depends on your definition of normal.

Is it just me or are there less and less numbers on buildings? I'll be driving down a street looking for an address, and often I don't see any addresses on the buildings, or if they are there, they're not any place you could spot them. Are they hiding them? Is there some point to not having the address on your building visible?

Also more and more the leaves on the trees are covering the signs on the highways, so you can't see where you are. And did streets and roads always just change their name as you drive straight ahead? What is the point? One road I occasionally drive on changes its name three times in twenty minutes. This is straight *ahead*! What's going on here? Is it me? Naah...I don't think it's me.

In those rare instances, when I've traveled, I've realized something you no doubt already know. Unpacking is a heck of a lot easier than packing. *Un*packing the job is right in front of you.

[131]

Packing? Well, that's a whole different story. I never seem to be able to figure out if it's hot or cold where I'm going and usually guess wrong. I always over pack to protect myself, and I *never* actually end up with what I need. I went to Florida on my last trip and didn't take a bathing suit. I guess that was my subconscious stepping up and saying "I don't really want to do this."

I saw a flying raft once, when I was on vacation. I told someone about it, and he said yeah, that's like a parasol – there's a line connected to a boat and it pulls you along about a hundred feet above the water. I said "No, it wasn't connected to *anything*. It was a raft with a motor with something that looked like a parachute above it, and it was flying pretty high up in the sky – maybe two football fields high – two hundred yards high – *high*! A flying raft." I don't know what they call what I'm calling a flying raft – but I've seen the future, and it was thrilling – not for *me*, of course.

I'm not a great flyer. I *really* want that drink before takeoff. This time I actually went out of turn to get it. I thought the guy wouldn't get to my row, before takeoff, so I motioned to him and went out of turn. It was pretty embarrassing.

A couple of people even turned and looked at me. Then, I phone ahead with my mattress requirement I spoke of earlier.

Very few people can follow what I'm talking about. It gets done, but not before at least one staff member and I have mini breakdowns. This trip, for reasons too complicated to go into, we went to *two* places in Florida, on opposite sides of the state. If anyone ever tells you, you can drive across the entire state of Florida in three hours, don't believe them. Not even close.

Of course, you *do* get to look at miles and miles of water filled ditches on both sides of the road, known as Alligator Alley. Of course, I phone ahead to the next place with the whole board, blanket routine.

Since when I get there, it's never done, I sometimes wonder if after talking on the phone to me, the hotel person quits. Once ensconced in the room, I seldom leave. I usually am arranging to receive a fax or a delivery of some kind. This involves several discussions with different sections of staff employed at this hotel.

I was told seven hundred people work there. We discuss several times how different things might be picked up and delivered. This is to put it mildly not a successful discussion, but everyone is *extremely* nice and *extremely* apologetic. I get the feeling some time I must be the only person in the world who's ever tried to get a delivery at a hotel. They make it sound so mysterious. "We have reason to believe the van might have left the location." What?!

At one point, in the middle of a mini breakdown I said, "You know this master bedroom has no window and the bed is so close to the closet, you have to stand sideways to get *in* the closet. " Everyone agreed, and soon I got a phone call from the manager, a really nice lady saying there was a possibility of us getting another place "1664," the lady said. I said, "Aw, we're not going to pay 1664 a night for a place to stay." She said, "No, that's the suite number." We did move.

It turned out to be great for everyone. For me, it didn't matter. I had been through too much. My wife and son and a support group of friends set off for the bumpy boat rides, fishing, shelling, ballooning, that kind of stuff. So in between trying to figure out delivery times, I lie on top of the board, (there's *never* enough blankets to keep it from feeling the board), but after a while, mercifully for everyone, I just stop talking about it. I lie there and write this stuff. It's actually a perfect job for me. I'd much rather write about vacations than take them.

There was a report that Swissair has decided to crack down on unruly passengers by having crew members tie them to their seats with plastic cords. At this point they deal with most people, who have had too much to drink and other out of control passengers by giving them a piece of paper warning them they can be prosecuted, when the plane lands. That usually gets people to put a lid on it but not always. The crew's union is against the idea of *tying people to their seats* but are negotiating the exact terms.

I guess the questions have to do with *when* you would tie someone to their seat? If they *shout?* If they *push someone? What?* Do you warn them? Do you say "You do that once more, and I'm going to tie you to your seat!" The idea of tying people on a plane to their seats is an interesting one but why stop at unruly passengers? Let's consider what to do with people, who talk so loudly on cell phones on planes that they're heard by rows of people around them, or people who talk that loudly, who aren't on cell phones. Maybe we don't have to tie them to their seats. How about just an adhesive gag there?

They could still get up and move around the cabin. They just wouldn't be able to talk. That seems fair. How about the captain, who wakes you from a sound sleep to let you know there's some mountain you might want to take a look at? Usually not on your side of the plane.

Turning off his mike for those observations, I think is enough there. What to do with people, who cause disturbances on planes is of course a serious issue, and I think the whole concept of tying unruly airline passengers to their seats is a good one, but it's only a nice beginning.

More and more I hear people say "I'm going to take a personal day." I assume that could be for a medical appointment, something to do with the kids, anything where you have your time to yourself…personal.

I find the personal days are the tough ones. I like work, more than personal days. Several years ago I took a vacation, which is a lot of personal days. I remember checking into this place, putting my bathing suit on, sitting in a chair on the beach, going to dinner, coming home, going to bed, getting up, going to breakfast, coming back to the room, putting on my bathing suit, sitting in a chair on the beach, and counting how long I had to stay there.

Someone once said to me "Live in the moment." I tried it, but it was really tough. Most of us are always *thinking* about a lot of stuff, so this living in the moment thing is harder than it sounds. The other day as a test, I tried just concentrating on a boat I could see in the distance.

I did it for about ten seconds, then I just started thinking about other stuff and wondering why I was staring at this boat in the distance? Someone said imagine where the boat came from, where it's going, and who's on it. I tried, but in a very short time I really didn't want to anymore. I just didn't care.

Another time a friend of mine got me to get in my car to quickly drive to this spot to see the sunset. It was very nice, and I understand if you took personal days you could watch the sun set *and* rise for that matter. But other than for a medical or family thing, I really don't want a personal day. Personally, I find personal days too demanding.

THE NEWS

"This glass of water may poison you."

When Michael Moore's documentary

Fahrenheit 9/11 came out, people loved it.
People hated it. It really nails President Bush.
It's incredibly unfair and untrue. There're *all*
kinds of opinions, but the one thing that's been
reported over and over *without* dispute is it got a
twenty minute ovation. I think they said
standing ovation.

Have you ever stood up or sat for that matter and
applauded for twenty minutes? Try *one* minute.
It will seem like forever. I haven't seen the film,
so I can't say what I think about it, but I'll tell
you with absolute certainty – there was *no*
twenty minute ovation. This was in *France* for
God's sake. There's a lot more to do there than
stand around and applaud for twenty minutes.

I'm not sure I understand why news anchors feel
they have to broadcast from the eye of a
hurricane. I saw CNN's Anderson Cooper
getting blown around. I've seen Dan Rather

years ago getting blown back and forth. Some of the anchors hold on to poles to keep from being blown off camera and maybe even out to sea. Is this about ratings? Would the ratings be lower, if the local guy was being blown around?

I don't remember Walter Cronkite ever being blown around in typhoon like winds. Maybe he was. Maybe I've just blocked it out of my mind. I like my anchors dry in a studio. Let the local guys have all the fun, if that's what it is. Personally I'm reluctant to go outside, if there's even a *chance* of rain.

I don't understand why there's so much laughter on local news casts and cable. There's rarely anything funny happening on the news, and yet there's all these people laughing away – sometimes almost doubled over in laughter.

You can definitely count on a lot of laughter around the weather report. When's the last time you found the weather funny? Look I like to laugh as much as the next guy, but when I see a lot of people laughing for no apparent reason, I have to tell you, it makes me tense.

These days the weather report is starting to get to me. *Way* too often, I'm sure to cover themselves the report seems to come with, showers or at least a *threat* of showers. "Sunny, warm, and clear – threat of showers." "A beautiful warm day tomorrow with a possible thunderstorm." "Tropical day, fog burning off in the morning – high in the 80's – chance of showers." One of my least favorite things is having hopes dashed. Sometimes I'd rather just have a cold day – well…not really, but that constant *threat* of showers is getting to me.

I like reading the New York Times. For the most part I think they write *up* to their readers. They understandably *expect* you to know that a demagogue is a person who appeals to the prejudices and emotions of people. Not *all* Times readers would know what a demagogue is.

Even less would know what a xenophobe is – hatred of strangers. They throw xenophobe around a lot in Times columns – not as much as demagogue but plenty. O.k. still with reasonable expectation they're not chasing their readers to dictionaries, *but* one day recently, they used demagogue, xenophobe *and* antediluvian in the same column. *Now* you're just showing off! I and I promise you thousands of other Times readers, who are always trying to improve themselves went to the dictionary on that one.

It means "the period before the biblical flood." So now we've learned something. I still say the Times writer was showing off. In fairness, my wife knew what antediluvian meant – but she went to Dartmouth. I mean – give me a break!

Over the years the 11 o'clock news has really made me nervous. Actually, it's not so much the 11 o'clock news as what they say is coming *up* on the 11 o'clock news. "Your pajamas could give you cancer. News at 11." This was actually a promo for the news I heard.

And you force yourself to stay up and you learn that what they're really saying is not *now*, but if they keep making pajamas with a certain thing in them, *later* your pajamas *may* give you cancer. A friend of mine went to a clothing store after that and asked if they had anything he could buy that wouldn't eventually kill him. "That glass of water you drank today may poison you. Coming up at 11."

Same thing. Turns out unless we stop polluting our water supply, *eventually* the water you drink *may* poison you. I can't really tell if I'm being poisoned right now, but it's sure not that unusual for me to feel a *little* funny. "Lack of sleep can be dangerous. Coming up at 11." Well, we all know about that. On the other hand, how are you supposed to relax and get a good night's sleep if you're worried about your pajamas giving you cancer.

I understand networks are sometimes in the business of promoting themselves, but has it ever been more overdone than it's currently being done on the Fox cable network? Fair and balanced, fair and balanced, fair and balanced. It feels like it's nonstop and between that you get we report you decide – *we report you decide* – we report you decide.

I haven't done a careful analysis of Fox, CNN or MSNBC, but I'll bet you've got fair and balanced reporting that lets you decide on all *three* networks, *and* biased journalism on all three as well. As far as which is the most fair and balance – well…you decide. Slogans are tricky. If you hear them too much, you start to get suspicious. I think I actually *believed* Avis *did* try harder, until I heard them say it too many times.

How would you like to be *live* on television several hours a day? Anderson Cooper of CNN is. I've seen him early in the morning when I get up and late at night when I go to bed. Live! Anderson Cooper is *always* live! I'm not sure *exactly* how *many* hours Anderson is live.

He probably eats and naps at certain points of the day, but whenever *I'm* watching he's either there or coming up. I wonder how many of *us* are up to being *live* on television several hours a day. It's not that *easy* to be *live* just around your own house.

I find it's getting tougher to shop. For several months now when I go into the drugstore to get an over the counter allergy medication – it's no longer over the counter – it's *behind* the counter.

You don't need a prescription, but you *do* have to show your driver's license, and *still* they will only sell you a limited amount. Evidently if you have enough of this stuff you can mix it up with other stuff and create *speed*. I assume speed is something that speeds you up, which believe me

is not something I'm looking to do. Relax?
Yes. Speed up? No.

Then if that wasn't enough, the other day I went
to the market and the checkout lady said "Hmm
you seem to be eating a lot of chicken." I said
"Yeah, well I uh uh…I mean it's *chicken*." I'm
not sure what to say. I don't personally feel I
have to *justify* eating chicken. I'm *not* using
speed, but I admit I eat a lot of chicken – wings,
legs, thighs. Hey! You know what? Leave me
alone! I'm *not* breaking any laws about chicken.

SELLING

"Give us a break with the selling."

I recently went to a food take-out place.

There was a bin marked beef stew. I got my container and began to scoop, but after four scoops which never made it into my container because there was *no* beef, I said to management "There's no beef. Where's the beef?" Management said there was someone in here yesterday who asked the same question. Well...I said if there's no beef in the beef stew it does beg the question?? You *must* have beef in your beef stew!

Some things are so counter-productive you have to wonder. Who's in charge here? I saw a commercial on television that first showed the ball player, Cal Ripken Jr. behind a table at a book signing. A young man, next on line approaches, seems to freeze with nerves and faints. Someone working in the bookstore runs over to him on the floor and shouts out to the crowd, "Did anyone stay at a Holiday Inn Express last night?"

A man leans in and identifies himself as a doctor. The bookstore guy ignores him and again shouts "Did anyone stay at a Holiday Inn Express last night?" It's an *ad* for Holiday Inn Express. *What*? It *seems* more like an ad *against* staying at a Holiday Inn Express – because you might faint or worse the next day.

Who's in charge there? *What* are you *saying*?! That's the way I feel about so much of what I hear these days. In fairness, I'm told if I had seen *a lot* of Holiday Inn ads, I would have understood the point, but I *haven't* seen a lot of Holiday Inn ads, so I'm left to assume if you stay at a Holiday Inn Express, you might faint the next day.

In case you don't have enough to worry about these days, I got a letter the other day asking for my support for an organization formed to prevent the collision of objects from outer space with earth. The organization wants to fund a "Traveling Near Earth Object Education Program."

Now for all I know this is very important. Maybe the collision of objects from outer space is as big a threat as say Terrorism or Mad Cow or Swine Flu – name your threat – but I'm just not up for this one.   I'm not saying there *isn't* a near earth collision threat.   I'm just kind of OD-ing on all the other threats.

I'm someone who's never liked to have my picture taken. Some people have found that odd, since I've spent so much of my life in show business. For all I know I'm *still* in it. I don't think I'm that unusual.

I'll bet a lot of you don't like to have your picture taken either. The other day in my local town paper I saw an ad for pre-natal photographs. The ad has a photo of a baby in a womb and says it's "A wonderful way to introduce family and friends to the new arrival." The company's called Looking In.

The removal of planet status for Pluto once again reminds me how tough it is to trust anything. It seems like it's a weekly event that endless thousands of cars are being recalled. Oh, we just realized they may *not* be safe.

Then there's all the medications that have been considered excellent for decades, until someone says, "Oh, wait a minute this could make your arm fall off." But to take away planet status from Pluto, which has been a planet for about eighty years, and now we only have eight planets instead of nine? I don't know...the whole removal of planet status for Pluto thing makes me less sure of things than ever.

I was in Mail Boxes Etc. the other day and there was a little dish of lollipops with different color wrappings on the counter. I picked out one with the grape wrapping, because I like grape, but when I took the wrapper off, the sucker was orange. It's amazing how often things just aren't what they seem to be.

Recently I went up to Mohican Sun, the gambling casino in Connecticut to see my friend Regis Philbin appear with his wife Joy. They put on a *great* show for about two thousand people. When I went to pick up my tickets it was very difficult to find the ticket window. I mean....it's miles of slot machines – casino tables etc. surrounded by entertainment venues.

When I was pointed in the right direction I still couldn't find the ticket window, so I went up to

[151]

a counter that said Coat Room. I said "Can you tell me where the ticket window is?" A lady said "*This* is the ticket window." I said, I *promise* you, very politely, "Maybe consider putting up a sign that says ticket window along with your coat room sign." She acted as though she hadn't heard me. For your own protection *never* underestimate the level of incompetence we're surrounded by in *all* fields.

I was going through the mail the other day, and I saw this check made out to me. I don't want to give the impression I never see a check in the mail, but it's a little unusual. Don't get me wrong – I *get* checks. It's just they seldom come directly to me, so I kind of enthusiastically opened the envelope to see whom it was from and for what and most importantly how much. Well it was for six hundred thousand dollars, but of course, it wasn't really a check, just some kind of come on that *looked* like a check. At the bottom of the check it actually had the words *"Not a check."* Oh, well.

If you were going to open a new restaurant, there obviously would be a lot to do including coming up with a name for it. So some people in India got together, and someone came up with the idea of calling their restaurant – Hitler's Cross, and while we're at it, let's put a swastika in the middle of the O for cross, just in case anyone misses that we're talking about *that* Hitler.

They did it! They put up the sign. Now there's only a very small Jewish community in India, but the protests were loud and clear. Initially the restaurant refused to change the name, I guess figuring they were getting a lot of free publicity. Well, of course, there's publicity and *publicity*. What were they thinking? Hitler as a selling tool? This was not supposed to be a place for only former and current Nazis to eat. Eventually they changed the name.

I've fallen twice in my life, both times on a slippery bathroom floor. This last time I sprained my ankle. We have a couple of throw rugs in the bathroom, but I asked the doctor why bathrooms don't have wall to wall carpeting?

He said "Wall to wall carpeting in a bathroom can cause mold." I got an A in Chemistry, but of course I have no idea why carpeting in a bathroom must cause mold. For you carpet makers out there. Make wall to wall carpeting for bathrooms that *doesn't* cause mold. You can do it! Maybe you already do.

We had some water damage in our house recently. Right about the same time I saw an ad on television that people can now get instructions from builders, for a fee I assume on how to do their own repairs.

They will teach you what you need to know about plumbing, putting up sheetrock, dry walling, etc. I'm sure this could be very cost saving for those who learn to do this on their own, but don't look at me, boss. Me? Dry walling? Sheet rocking?   I don't think so.

It's been flattering all these years to receive fan mail, but I read recently that someone said "He no longer responds to fan mail asking for a picture or autograph, because he realized they're being sold." I asked my assistant to go on line to see if she could purchase an autographed photo of me.

She did, and told me there were several from different movies at different prices, so I will no longer respond to fan mail or open it. However,

I will continue to believe all those past possibly *false* compliments. Hey! Whatever works.

This keeps happening to me, so I going to assume it happens to at least *some* of you. I can't open things. In the past and present it's mostly been pills like Advil Cold and Sinus, I can't get out of their enclosure. I eventually can do it, but at this stage of life, I shouldn't have to work that hard to take a pill.

Now for the first time it's the tab you have to pull off of the large container of orange juice. I *couldn't* pull it off. Not to brag, but I was an undefeated boxer, all right, as a *teenager*, but I've got *some* strength. Eventually I tried to pull it off with my teeth. The tab broke, but didn't open. Then I had to stab my way in to get at the juice. *People* before you sell something make sure it's user friendly, or at least user *possible*.

I realize the publishing business isn't what it used to be, but I was still very surprised the other day when I went to a friend's book party, where they generally give you the book – and now they were *charging* for it, even urging you to *buy* several copies. I told another friend about it, and he said *eight years ago*, he went to a book party where the author, a friend of his signed the book to him.

As he was leaving someone followed him and asked for payment. If you have to depend on *friends* to make your book a decent seller...well... I hope this doesn't portend a time in the future where you're invited to someone's house for dinner and they bill you. *Naah...*

The other day while driving into Manhattan I saw a sign put up by the Manhattan Mini Storage Company. It said "Storing at your parents' means having to visit." No doubt it was meant to be humorous, but I wasn't amused.

Children of *all* ages have problems with their parents and parents of all ages have problems with their children of all ages – but overwhelmingly as great a *bond* as any is between parents and children. If that doesn't apply to you, maybe you need to take a harder look at yourself, unless your dad was Jack the Ripper.

This or something *like* this can't just be happening to me. I was suddenly getting a lot of static on a little radio I have. I asked a guy at Radio Shack, if that meant I needed new batteries. He said "No. When batteries aren't good, the radio doesn't play."

Given my experience with all knowing people I went home and put in new batteries. The static immediately stopped. Then I bought some baby aspirin. When I went to open it – it said "Easy twist off top." *You* can finish that story.

It's more and more difficult to say "Just when I thought I'd heard everything." The Barnes and Noble book chain is now offering back to school *hair*cuts and *flu shots*. Next we'll hear about barber shops and doctor's offices selling books. Hey…times really *are* tough.

It seems everywhere I go these days – the market – the drugstore – just about *any* store, the cashier asks me if I have a discount card – or a membership card – or some kind of card. When I say I don't, they'll tell me the advantages of having one – they're free – you get coupons in the mail, and after a hundred dollars-worth of purchases or something like that – I start getting

[157]

discounts, if I present my coupons. Since like a lot of you, I'm sure, I'm already drowning in paper – I say "No thanks. Thanks a lot. That's o.k."

Now I'm hearing about a place – Costco – this huge warehouse that looks like it sells everything from tooth brushes to *cars*, where you can't even get *in*, unless you're a member. This isn't a private club where you'd expect it; it's a *warehouse* for Pete's sake. In the coming years, am I going to have to be a member before I can get myself a lamb chop?

It's most gratefully *less,* since I signed up for the Do Not Call list, but *some* still get through. They often start off the same way. "Hello, is this Charles?" They're not calling me, because they know who I am. I'm just some guy on a list named Charles.

Just about any time you buy something these days, they want to know your name and phone number. This is what it leads to. The people who call at dinnertime and begin by saying "This is a courtesy call" are *really* annoying. Sometimes the calls are a recording "Hi! This is Jennifer at the resort center. You have been invited..." Somehow I actually enjoy hanging up on a recording.

A friend of mine said when a salesperson calls and asks for him, he says he's out of the country for six months. Someone said when they call, just tell them to take your number of the list, and that's what I've been doing lately, and people are very nice, and say they will. The calls keep coming though, so there must be *a lot* of lists.

It's not always that simple. A lady called recently and said "Is this Charles?" I said "Who's calling?" She gave her name and the name of some company. I said "Would you take my number off your list?" She again asked "Is this Charles?"

I said again "Would you please take my number off the list?" She again said very nicely "Is this Charles?" I said "We really don't take calls from people we don't know." She *again* asked "Are you Charles?" I then said "Why do you want to know?" She said "I just want to know if you're Charles?" I was starting to feel like I was back in sixth grade. I said "Please take our number off your list." She *then* said "Have a nice day."

[159]

It was certainly nicer *after* the call. So *many* people who tell you to "Have a nice day" do nothing to help that happen. The other day I answered the phone, and a young woman said "Hello, is this Charles?" and started selling me something.

I interrupted her and said, "Would you take our number off the list?" She said "Okay." Then there was a pause, as though she expected me to say more, so I said very nicely "I get calls like this all day long." She said "Well, they're not all from *us*." I said, "I realize that, but I'm sure you can understand to get these calls every day…" She hung up on me.

One thing all of us have in common is being kept on hold on the telephone. Surveys have shown we spend about twenty five percent of our lives sleeping. It's certainly not *that* long on hold, it just *feels* like it sometimes. These days before you're put on hold, you hear the menu.

And before you hear the *menu*, you hear this, if for example, you call American Airlines to find out if an arriving flight's on time. "Thank you for calling American Airlines, a proud member of the One World Alliance. Your call may be monitored or recorded to ensure quality service. In addition to the fare information you receive on this call, American may offer lower fares through one of our internet partners, or on our own website at www.aa.com." *Then* you get press one for this and two for that and three and four, and five and six and seven for different things, and *then* you're on hold.

I don't know, maybe I'm not remembering this right, but I think there was a time a person would answer the phone and say "American Airlines." I'd say, "Hi, is flight 623 from Chicago on time?" There'd be a short pause and they'd say, "Yes, it is at Gate 42." I say "Thanks" and that was it!

For me, the *worse* hold situation is when a recording keeps telling you how important your call is to them, but no one picks up to ask what the heck you're calling about. Your call is very important to us. We really value you as a customer, so please stay on the line. We even like your hair."

I called a restaurant the other day, and while I was on hold they kept telling me how important

I was, and then they told me how wonderful they *were*. "We have the finest cuisine. Excellent service at reasonable prices. You will dine in a simple, yet elegant décor." I started talking back to the recording. "I know. I heard about you. That's why I'm calling. I *heard* about the décor!"

I called my doctor's office the other day, and while you're on hold, you hear a radio station. A commercial eventually came on for life insurance. I know I'm being too sensitive, but when I call my doctor's office, I don't want to hear a commercial for life insurance.

To all the people out there who are in charge of what goes on your hold recording, I would ask you to give some thought to the entertainment value of your hold message. If we're holding past the time when you've put out whatever you think is your necessary information, in my case, I'd then appreciate hearing Frank Sinatra singing *New York, New York* or maybe something by Perry Como.

I'll bet plenty of people still respond to this kind of stuff. I got something in the mail labeled *"official notice"* from a business of some kind.

It gave me a toll free number and said: "Dear C. (That's how they referred to me – C.) We are trying to reach you regarding your one million dollar sweepstakes. (One million bucks!) Please call us at the above number. This is a free call." I'll bet plenty of people call. Too bad.

I can't really call these two things pet peeves, because they bother me more than just a peeve, even more than a *pet* peeve. The first more than pet peeve is how people use the word "fact" in their efforts to persuade. You see it on cable shows a lot or probably anywhere people are trying to sell their points of view. People say "That's a fact" or "Those are the facts" when they're *not* the facts or at least the *"facts"* are in dispute. Most people who live together see the "facts" differently, so it's tough to get the whole viewing audience to accept your "facts."

We expect that people try to sell us things on radio and television. In recent years there are commercials, when you go to the movies. People try to sell us things by sky writing and even on the floors of some markets. It's getting harder to find a cap or a shirt that doesn't advertise or have someone's name on it.

The other day as I scooped the last bit of instant coffee from the jar, there was a piece of paper in there telling me how good the coffee was. It also raved about their new lid. I realize none of this is new, but it's starting to make me more than average edgy.

It's been a long time since I worked in sales. When I was in college I worked briefly as a shoe salesman, but I must have been pre-occupied as more than once I unfortunately misplaced the shoes the customer wore *into* the store. Over the years like most of us I've become a little wary of salespeople – the ones who kind of aggressively approach you anyway, because…well they're trying to *sell* you something.

This past Monday, all these years later, I became a salesperson again. We were hit by a blizzard in the Northeast, and the feeder in our backyard was getting plenty of business, but there were still plenty of birds and squirrels rummaging around in the snow.

I had put some pieces of bread out there, but they immediately sunk into the snow. I decided to put some pieces of crackers on a *tray*, so they wouldn't immediately sink. I shut the door, looked through the curtain on the window and waited.

Nobody came – not *one* squirrel – not *one bird*. I suddenly began to feel like an unsuccessful salesman. I had put out a good product. It was even *free,* and I couldn't get one customer. I began to think of all the salespeople waiting, knowing they have a good product, and no one comes to buy it. Eventually after a longer time than I imagined, the buyers, the squirrels and birds came and cleaned out the inventory. But the whole experience gave me an increased empathy for all salespeople.

I realize it's necessary to properly seal boxes before shipping something, but honestly I think sometimes people over do it. I had something shipped to me the other day that was sealed with so much tape, it took me a good ten minutes to get it open. First I tried to use a letter opener to break into it. That didn't really work, so I just began to stab at it – anything to create an opening.

That didn't really work either. It's not that extraordinary that *I* end up with a cut or two on my fingers. Don't get me wrong. I believe in sealing, but there's sealing, and then there's *sealing*! Give us a break with the sealing.

I never take the receipts when I buy something, toothpaste, food anything! Like most of you I'm already drowning in paper. I pay for just about everything with a credit card, so I figure my credit card statement is my receipt, if the government decides to question me. The other day after I told the woman at the cash register I didn't want the receipt, she said "Are you sure?"

Up until now, everyone's just said "O.k." but this woman asked me, if I'm *sure* I don't want the receipt. I said I *was* sure. Then I started to think about how many other things I *was* sure about *other* than not wanting the receipt. It's a very short list. I'm sure I love my wife, and kids, and friends. Although there is one guy I'm not *so* sure about.

As I always say, I'm sure I'd rather stay home than travel. My son asked me incredulously the other day "You mean there's *nowhere* you'd like to go?" I said "No, I'll just stay home." So I'm sure about the receipts and my love of family and friends except for that one guy I mentioned, and I'm sure I want to stay home. Other than that, I'm not *so* sure about anything.

I think I was about twelve years old when all us kids had to take what used to be called aptitude tests. Basically the results indicated I should be an accountant. The fact that I had less than no interest whatsoever in accounting, I guess didn't show up on the test.

While I did fine in most areas, the test also showed that I was in the lowest one twelfth of the nation in mechanical and electrical aptitude. I don't know whether understanding written instructions comes under mechanical, I doubt it, so I think the test missed another lowest one twelfth area for me, because I really have a heck of a time understanding written instructions.

Talk to me and I get it. Write down instructions, I'm lowest one twelfth. This all came to mind recently when I applied for an E-Z Pass sticker so I can drive my car through toll booths, be automatically charged and not wait on line to pay cash. It arrived with a lot of literature. Maybe my mistake is I actually read some of this stuff. On the back of it, it said "This device may not cause harmful interference, and it must

[167]

accept any interference received including interference received that may cause undesired operation." I really don't know what that means.

I guess it means it can't cause interference with driving, but how do I know if it's going to cause interference? I'm sure it won't. Otherwise I hope someone would stop them from selling it to us. I mean why is that written there?!

Then there's this thing that says "Keep this pouch in your glove compartment," and then it says "to avoid your tag being read by E-Z Pass, place your tag in this pouch and fold it over." What? Why? What is this? Keep it in your glove compartment in a pouch, so no one can see it?! What's it for?

Then I go to the booklet. I can't help myself. I've got about another minute of this, before I can't do it anymore, and I really would *like* to know what they're talking about. I may be in the lowest one twelfth in understanding this stuff, but I still try.

I open the booklet to the chapter on How to Install Your Interior E-Z Pass Tag, and immediately spot an illustration of a guy doing it, that *really* depresses me, because he looks so *happy*, as though he knows what he's doing. Clearly he's in the *top* one twelfth in this department. I close the booklet and figure I'll come back to it later when I feel better, but honestly…I know that will never happen.

I was reading the ingredients on a bottle of Gatorade the other day, because that's just the kind of guy I am. Here's what they are: water, sucrose syrup, glucose fructose syrup, citric acid, natural lemon and lime flavors with other natural flavors, salt, sodium citrate, monopotassium phosphate.

Now I don't really know what monopotassium phosphate is, but o.k. I'll go with it, but the *last* two ingredients are ester gum and yellow 5. Hold it right there! Ester gum and yellow 5. C'mon! I'm going to assume *somebody* out there knows what ester gum and yellow 5 are, and they're okay, but *really*. Ester gum and yellow 5?!

We know that *people* can guilt provoke each other, but *magazines*?! The other day I saw an envelope from Vanity Fair magazine reminding my wife to renew her subscription. My wife sends certain magazines to her mother, and on the envelope from Vanity Fair it said "Don't disappoint" and then it had my wife's mother's name. *Magazines* are trying to make us feel guilty?!

We see sexual overtones everywhere these days, but on cereal?! I was looking at a package of Granola the other day. It's called Bare Naked. It's actually spelled Bar Naked, there are some lines after the B in Bar and after K in naked, but no question it's meant to communicate bare naked.

It also says on the package "Fuel your wild life." It also says "Do you get Bar Naked? We do." I guess everyone gets bare naked at some point or another, but is it the kind of thing we're supposed to focus on while eating cereal?

I wonder how many wonderful economic opportunities I'm missing when I go to a market or a drug store, they ask me something like "Am I a golden gift card holder"? I say "No," They say "Would you like to be?" I again say "No." I don't even ask what a golden gift card is, how much money it could save me, I don't ask anything. I just say no.

Also I can barely carry all the advertisements that daily come in the mail now, and I'm *sure* every time I sign up for *anything*, here comes more pounds of mail. I may be missing out on a lot of economic opportunities but for me – as my mother would say, "It's *enough* already!"

Have you seen this guy who comes on television for 1-800 lawyers? He's telling you to call 1-800 lawyers for…if you need a lawyer. What a *look* this guy has – jet black hair – big jet black mustache – piercing eyes – a really scary looking guy. I assume he's an actor. I guess the people who picked him wanted a guy who could look that scary to get you to call them for a lawyer. I guess that's obvious. That's what you want. A real scary looking guy for a *lawyer*.

As I'm sure you know, there are a number of people who are paid to appear on television as experts on this or that. These people are under *contract* to appear, so it always makes me smile, when the host thanks them profusely for appearing. "Thank you so much. I really appreciate your taking the time from your busy schedule to be here etc. etc."

These people are *paid* to be there. They're *expected* to be there just like you or I am, if we go to work. Does anyone thank *you* profusely for showing up for your paid job? I don't *think* so.

The traveling Antique Road Show that I sometimes catch on television gets my attention. There's always a dealer talking to the owner of some antique about how it has this inlay and that original molding, when the owner and we as the audience are just waiting to hear *"What's it worth!"* The other day a dealer was doing this about an antique cat with a big fish in its mouth. It was the original cat. It was the original fish etc. etc. *How much*??!!

We know about teams selling naming rights to stadiums. We know you can name a star after someone with the star registry – for a fee, of course. Now they're selling naming rights to a rare monkey somewhere. Some new kind of monkey was discovered and somehow the discoverer or whoever is selling naming rights. For the right amount of bucks, I bet you could name him Fred – if you wanted. Truth really is stranger than fiction.

We got this new refrigerator. They just couldn't
stop the hum from the old one. I mean
supervisors came to the house and tried, and
they couldn't stop the hum, so we got a new one
– an upgrade – *theoretically*!

In the sense that it doesn't *hum* all day, it *is* an
upgrade, but you can't attach photos to it with
magnets – you know all the kids in *your* family
and *your* relative's kids. Your friend's kids –
you can't attach the kids to the refrigerator.
Also if you open and close the freezer door, you
can't open it again for what *feels* like an
unfathomable length of time. Why? I ask you?
Why? This is an *upgrade*?! I miss the hum.

If there's one subject I've thought about as much
as anything, it's how difficult it is to get at a pill
enclosed in plastic. Recently I came across a pill
that was not only seemingly glued closed, but
came in a box that nowhere said how often you
were supposed to take that pill, *if* you could ever
get it *out* of its enclosure. The box was mostly
warnings about what could happen to you, if you
took this pill. Maybe they didn't even *want* you
to take it.

If you're selling a pill almost impossible to get at that comes in a box telling all the terrible things that can happen to you if you take it – it's *possible* they want you to *buy* it, but not actually *take* it, because of possible lawsuits.

I mean it says on the box this pill could give you hives, give you a rash – even put you in shock! After reading all this I saw up in the corner of the box – lift here for more drug facts. Once after *much* effort you peel *that* back – you learn you're supposed to take this pill, that could put you in shock every four hours. Needless to say, I didn't take it. The best idea is let's just not get sick.

The other day I went to a hardware store and bought three cans of paint – some brushes and some other stuff you need if you're going to paint something. The clerk asked me "Would you like a bag?" I looked at him a second to see, if he was serious. He was, so I said "Yes, thank you." I get that question more and more these days. "Would you like a bag?" Have you ever seen someone carrying six items in their hands, under their arms? Would we like a bag? Yes, we'd like a bag. I don't get it.

I was at a fund raiser for a very worthy cause the other night. Part of the way they raised money was to have an auction, and one of the items being auctioned off was dinner with a gorgeous young woman, who had won a big national beauty contest.

When her name was called she appeared as a vision from the audience and took the stage beside the auctioneer. I have to believe there weren't that many well to do *single* men in the audience, because the bid started and ended at five hundred dollars. The beautiful young woman never stopped smiling, *until* she left the stage, and then her face dropped. Five hundred dollars to have dinner with one of the most beautiful women in the world. Don't let yourself be auctioned off. The price may be so low, you'll never get over it!

I'm a big fan of doo wop – the songs from the early days of rock and roll. Artists like Lightning Lou Christie, Little Anthony and the Imperials, singers like that take me back to a more peaceful time, and I love it. I often see concerts featuring these singers on public broadcasting, and you can order a DVD or cassette of the concerts. The other day I saw an ad for a concert being promoted as Doo Wop gold. It said if you call in the next ten minutes – you could get it for half price. I kind of trotted to where my credit card was – came back – dialed the number so quickly. I *miss dialed* twice. Hey! Who doesn't like a bargain?

Finally I got a young woman on the phone. She took my order, my name, phone number, address, and credit card number, and that's when it started. She offered me about six different other "opportunities." I kept saying "No thanks. I just want the Doo Wop gold." "How about this etc, etc.?" No thanks. I just want the Doo Wop gold. Over and over. I just want the Doo Wop gold.

This went on for so long I chose not to interrupt her, to see how far she'd go. Finally she seemed to accept that in *fact,* I *did* just really want the Doo Wop gold. Then she said as *part* of the Doo Wop gold offer I was going to be sent a *free* two month subscription to about eight magazines she rattled off. I said I didn't want any more magazines – even if they *were* free – which I doubted. She said o.k. and *then* she started to talk about some contingency where I'd also be sent – I *forget* what – because I just couldn't listen anymore!

I did hear enough to know that along with my Doo Wop gold I would be sent a form to fill out, if I wanted to *stop* them sending me whatever else they were going to send me. At that point – I asked her I hope politely to forget about the whole thing. I think I said something like I just wanted the Doo Wop gold – I had no intention of going into business with you. I was surprised when she very easily said o.k., and the call mercifully came to an end.

At the beginning of the whole thing they say something about the conversation being monitored for quality control. They should *start* their quality control, by looking at the amount of things the young woman was instructed to try to sell me. I can't be the *only* customer who will walk away, if you try to sell them everything in the *store*!

This is another example of hearing more than you ever wanted to know. We had a leak in our basement recently, and the fella the plumbing company sent out to fix it somehow made the

[177]

phones stop working. He explained to me how that happened. He got about two sentences in – something about circuit breakers and I said, "Please, please, I won't be able to follow any of this! Please stop." I might even have said "I beg you."

Later he explained it to my wife, who also had no interest but is more gracious than I am, I guess. On another subject, but the same theme is something I heard on a baseball broadcast the other night. I'd have to say sports is right up there with the things that get my attention, but when an announcer asked a pitcher "Now when you release the ball on that pitch what fingers touch the ball last?" I felt I was back in my basement with the plumber feeling "Let me out of here!" There *is* such a thing as *too* much information.

Today I do most of my work at home, but since I don't live alone, and my wife doesn't share my feelings about travel, every so often I find myself *not* at home, but somewhere *else*. It's usually a very nice place, but it's not home. The weather is always better there, but I don't rate weather very high up on my conditions for happiness. So whenever I find myself away from home, I try to find some humor in what I don't care for.

For example, on my recent vacation I was consistently asked by this very upbeat fella who was in charge of guest relations, how everything was, and while I could point out a few flaws with the place – little things like you can't really see the floor numbers to push on the elevator, without bending over and getting real close to them – I chose never to mention that or *anything* else – like you can't really turn around in the shower without almost hitting your nose, and I have a relatively small nose.

But one day I decided to answer the question "Is everything alright?" *honestly* – so I said "Please don't take this as a complaint – just an observation – but I'm not sure you want to have someone with a loud power saw sawing off branches on trees outside your window at 7 a.m." My guest relations pal just stared at me and slowly repeated what I said just to make sure he heard right. I smiled and said he had. I'll take the power saw any day just to see the look on his face. As I've said, under any and all circumstances, whenever possible, look for the laugh.

I guess it's a few years now, since I've stopped
finding it strange that I'm asked my home phone
number when I drop a pair of pants off at the
cleaners, or do they ask when I pick them up, or
at both times? Then, of course, they ask my
address. I guess all this is to verify it's me, and
I'm not some guy trying to get someone else's
pants. I guess. At Radio Shack where I
sometimes go to get a few batteries, they need to
know my phone number and address. Why?
Again, to make sure it's me? You wouldn't
expect them to sell batteries to just anyone,
would you?

I heard the other day on the radio about a survey
that said if you aggressively tell someone to do
something most people will do it. It didn't say
do what, but the survey sounded right to me. I
mean when people ask for all this information
they don't even do it aggressively. They just
ask, and we tell.

I guess it seems easier than saying "Why do you
want to know?" I did that once to a clerk in a
hardware store, and he backed off immediately,
but there was an unpleasant tension between us

after that. The next time I'm there I'll probably just give up the info.

I can imagine a time when I buy a Snickers candy bar, and the salesperson after getting the basic data on me will say "You used to buy Milky Ways, why the change?" I'll then say "Snickers has nuts"! The clerk will note that in the computer and then say "So sometimes you prefer nuts?" "Yes," I'll say, and then they'll say "By the way what is your mother's maiden name?"

The other day I was looking at a confirmation letter from a hotel where I had recently made a reservation. It said there was a 7% state tax and a 6% occupancy tax, which I took to mean you could knock 6% of the charge for the room if you didn't actually *stay* in it. I know people are always trying to cut back on expenses, but *that* sure didn't seem like the best way to do it.

I wanted to get a sport jacket pressed the other day, so I stopped in a cleaners and asked if they could do it while I waited. The lady said come back in ten minutes, and they'd have it for me. When I did she said "That will be $4.50." I handed her a ten.

She said "What's your phone number?" I said "My phone number? I don't want to give you my phone number. Can't I just pay you?" She said no, because in order to open the cash register, she'd needed my phone number. I said "What if I gave you four singles and fifty cents, and you put it in when you already had the register open for another customer?" She said she'd have to check with the manager, who eventually o.k.'d it. What is this all *about*?!

Over the years I've bought countless humidifiers, which I've either thrown away or returned to this big national chain store that sells them. I always ask if anyone else's humidifier ever stops working, and they always say with a straight face and sincerity too "We've never had a return of this humidifier." They're very polite.

Recently they gave me a different brand of humidifier, which costs less and a credit slip for the difference. Very nice except I couldn't help but notice the young lady doing the paper work at her computer was on her *knees*.

I asked her "Why are you on your knees?" She said it hurts her back to bend over the computer.

I figure if no one in this big place suggests putting the computer higher or giving the young lady a chair – how much of an eye are they keeping on the humidifier end of the business? Just asking.

Also, I keep buying these silent humidifiers that make noise. Not only that but just like a lot of items these days, they're filled with symbols, whose meanings are known only to the people who put them there.

One of my silent humidifiers makes so much clicking and strangling sounds I can only keep it on, if I'm not home. I'm positive they only stay in business, because they sell towels and other cloth items. Cloth doesn't make noise, and it does the job, like only cloth can. I could easily open a discount humidifier store for the hearing impaired.

You'd *have* to really be hearing impaired not to hear the steady beeping sound that goes along with the loud hissing sound on my newest quietest humidifier on the market. Right on the side it says "Call this 800 number before using." From past experience I really try to avoid calling those 800 numbers, so I just turned the humidifier on, but after a few minutes of beeping and hissing, I called the 800, and spoke to a recording *of course*, which asked me to say and then spell my name, my address, my zip code, my phone number etc. etc.

After a few minutes of me and the recording talking over each other, I hung up and wondered if I just stared at the thing – a *hard stare* for a minute or so, things might improve. They didn't. I called the store and after getting disconnected a few times, an incredibly smart woman came on and instructed me how to program a *remote* to rid the thing of the beeps. Eventually I got the beeps to go away, and I've only got the loud hissing. In some strange way it feels like a triumph. And this is the *quietest* humidifier! It should come with ear plugs.

This whole I.D. thing can get a little strange. In certain obvious instances it seems entirely appropriate to be asked for I.D. *but*…The other day I went into Toys R Us to return a video game for my nephew, that didn't work. It turned out that none of their other copies worked either. I had the receipt, and they were going to issue me a store credit, but first they wanted to see my driver's license, I guess to make sure I didn't *steal* the defective copy and receipt from some other customer. My license was in my car, so they gave me a good once over and then issued the credit. I think the next time something like that happens and they want to see my driver's license, I'm going to ask to see *their* driver's license.

I can't even keep a list of all the things I buy at the drug store that I have to show photo I.D. for. Next it will be proof of citizenship. I'm talking about allergy medication, Sudafed etc. They look at me like I might be heading a major drug ring.

Most of you know this, but evidently someone has figured out how to make stuff we've routinely taken for years like to stop sneezing into *illegal* drugs. It's an underground drug business. I promise you that's *not* what I'm doing. I'm *just* trying to stop sneezing, and I'm all but fingerprinted. What a world.

Those calls you get at home with people selling you something were supposed to go away if you signed up for that national do not call list which I did. There's certainly less of them, but every so often I still get one.

The other day the phone rang and the conversation literally went like this. I say literally because it was short, and I wrote it down. I changed the name of the woman, because I'm not out to embarrass anyone here.

She said, "This is Janice with Preferred Rate." I immediately interrupted what I knew was the oncoming pitch by asking, "What's Preferred Rate, Janice?" There was a short silence and then Janice said "Uh…you'll have to ask my supervisor. Can I ask you a few questions to see if you qualify?" "Naah," I said. Janice said "Oh. Thanks. Goodbye." So they've got people selling you Preferred Rate who don't know what Preferred Rate is. I'll tell you this though. I feel a lot worse for Janice, than I do for me.

This definitely comes in the category of you gotta be kidding. There was something called the Kleenex couch, which is touring eight cities across America. An actor playing a therapist sits on a chair and asks any willing passerby, if they would like to sit down and answer some questions.

In this case, this in New York City on Broadway and Forty Fifth Street. The questions are meant to elicit emotional responses, and they do.

One woman spoke about how sad she was about the loss of her husband's mother. A nineteen year old student from Florida said "I let everything out and just started to cry. I felt weird crying in front of a total stranger, but he didn't judge me. He just let me talk to him."

All this belongs in the "you gotta be kidding" category, because it's a *commercial* for Kleenex which will be shown on Kleenex's letitout.com and the best clips may make it onto t.v. I'm sure the participants signed releases, but if they aren't also paid, if the footage is used – then you've *really* got to be kidding.

If you go to www.TalkToAliens.com you can find a phone number that lets you leave a message for any extraterrestrials who might be out there. The calls cost $3.99 a minute. Two questions; how many people have done this, and how long has this company been in business? If the numbers are significant, we may have more problems than I thought.

I would never claim to be someone who has never had any problems to overcome. It's just that my *weight* has *not* been one of them. Nevertheless I received something in the mail recently – a card. The headline said "Today's your lucky day, Charles Grodin. Then it said "Charles, have these obstacles *prevented* you from losing weight?" It was an ad for discounts on different workout equipment. It even gave me my own *secret* code to contact them.

Fellas, fellas, fellas, I don't have a weight issue. I *have* workout equipment. I'm not saying I *use* it, but I *have* it. *Sometimes* I use it. So leave me alone on your discounts on equipment. Of course, if you have any ideas on how to make the world a better place – please contact me *immediately*. I won't even ask for a discount.

Food markets seem to be getting bigger and bigger which I'm sure some people must like, because it gives them more choices. Not me! There're so many choices I can't *find* anything! I wander up and down aisles. The sign says I'm in the right aisle, but there are so *many* cereals.

Whatever, I just can't find the one I'm looking for. *Worse*, neither can the poor people working there, who mercifully try to help me. Not fun. Frustrating – exhausting. Do we really need seventy kinds of everything?

I'm fascinated by the radio ads where people call the Men's Warehouse clothing store to leave a message for the owner *and* founder George something. They're always *raving* about their new jacket or suit and the marvelous treatment they received at the warehouse.

When was the last time you left a message at a clothing store raving about how much you loved your new suit? I'm not saying these people *don't* love their new whatever, I'm just saying I'm *fascinated* all these people keep leaving messages at the store *saying* they do.

POLITICS

"Who are these people with all these plans?"

I had a meeting with the Speaker of the House of Connecticut once and while I was talking to him, someone pinned a small fancy medallion on my jacket lapel. When I got home, I took it off and looked at it. It had I assume Latin words on it. I studied Latin in high school, but I wouldn't swear it's Latin. It's *probably* Latin. It said *Qui Transtulit Sustinet.*

I asked my son to check it out on his computer. It's the Connecticut state motto. It means "He who transplanted still sustains." I mean even in *English,* I don't know what it means. Do you think Connecticut or *any* state should have a motto, where I promise you *maybe* a tiny percentage of people know what it means. I don't think so. I suggest "He who preservers will more likely prevail," and let's say it in *English.*

I was listening to a politician being interviewed the other day, and I was again struck by how long politicians talk to answer the simplest of questions. A question like "Do you think you'll run again?" is answered by paragraphs of verbiage. The saying "A battleship of words to launch a row boat of thought" comes to mind. You hardly ever simply hear yes, no or even maybe from a politician. I also keep thinking of the word "obfuscation," which according to Webster means "making things obscure, or confusing."

That may be the thing a lot of politicians are best at. It *feels* like their hope is to wear us down, so we'll forget what the question was or at least lose interest in the subject, so they can go about their business, whatever that may be, unimpeded by a lot of irritating questions.

I have one friend, who's *not* a politician, who talks like that. I was once watching a Little League baseball game, where his son was pitching. He showed up in the third inning, looked at the scoreboard, which showed his son's team behind by four runs and asked me "Were there any defensive opportunities that weren't taken advantage of?"

It took me a minute, before I realized he wanted to know if his son was giving up hits or his team was making errors in the field. "Were there any defensive opportunities that weren't taken

[193]

advantage of?" Because of his not wanting to point fingers at others, I found his obscure way of talking charming. I wish I felt the same way about the politicians.

If you were running for office, you'd probably have to come up with a bumper sticker of some kind. National office probably wouldn't be too hard. "Keeping America Strong" I think works nicely. Local town office is tougher. The other day I saw a bumper sticker for a guy running for a local office. It said his name, and then it said "Standing up for you."

I don't think that works. Who's you? You're standing up for me? How do you know what I want you to stand up for me *for*? Since most of the people I know in my town pretty much don't agree about *anything*, I just don't think "Standing up for you" works.

Political spin is a wonderful thing to behold. In the world of political spin, there is never any bad news. If you're indicted on forty six federal counts of misuse of funds, taking bribes, lying to investigators, etc. you say "Finally I have a chance to clear my name against all these false charges and vicious innuendos. When the truth emerges, I expect to be fully exonerated." After conviction?

"Of course, I plan to appeal. When certain facts are allowed into evidence, truth will ultimately be served, and justice will prevail. God bless America. In the meantime, good wishes and checks can be sent to my website c/o Sing Sing.com."

I thought about all of this years ago when Vermont's Senator Jim Jeffords defected from the Republican party, handing control of the Senate to the Democrats. Objective political observers, if there is such a thing, would have to say this is not good news for the president and his party, but some spinners still sprang into action with things like "The Republican party is better off. Jeffords was never one of us anyway," or "Now we'll see the Democrats for the obstructionists they really are, as they think of one way after the other to stymie the President's program."

If you listen to this stuff long enough, you begin to think "Wow, what a break for the Republicans! If Senator McCain leaves, they'll *really* have it made."

Of course, this latest Republican spin still has to take a back seat to former President Clinton's spin, after he was forced to admit to a relationship with Monica Lewinsky; "Even a President is entitled to a private life." But as time goes by the real spin golden oldies no doubt will be these Clinton favorites; "It depends on what your definition of 'is' is," followed by his ever popular "It depends on how you define "alone."

Saddam Hussein spun for years that he really won his war with us. After all even the first president Bush once said of Saddam "He's still got a job and I don't." Slobodan Milosevic spun for years that he won the war in Kosovo with us as well. He pointed out he was still in power and more popular than ever with his people for standing up to the super power villain United States.

The spin even seemed to work, until his people voted him out of office, then stormed his house and threw him into a small cell. Sometimes even for the best *spinners*, it gets a little tough to spin.

Whatever you may think of the last President Bush, I must say I was always a bit taken aback, when I saw him strutting around. Personally I could do without the strutting, but I have to give him this – you never heard "President Bush is indisposed."

Oh, there was that time once when we were told he fainted after choking on a pretzel, but other than that – strutting. With everything a president has to deal with you could understand, if he *was* more often indisposed. So whatever we may think of the strutting, at least he was *out* there strutting when you could easily imagine he's behind closed doors being given sedatives.

I was elected president eight times in high school (we had elections every six months). Even though I'd win every time I ran, I do not feel qualified to run for *any* office. I've been happily married for a long time, even though I don't cheat or even *flirt* – even though I have no skeletons in my closet, I am not qualified to run for *any* office.

Even though I *too* am confident I could shake my head negatively and smile knowingly as my opponent is talking, I'm not qualified. Even though I'm sure I could *appear* to master every subject as well as my opponent can *appear* to – I am *not* qualified to run for office.

The reasons I'm not qualified are simple. You have to leave your house *a lot* – endlessly travel, endlessly ask people for money and sit in long boring meetings for what I'm sure feels like forever! You have to be willing to do that, and I'm *not willing.* I am *really* not willing. In order to be qualified to run for office, the first requirement is you have to *want* to. And, I don't *want* to!

They say that speaking in public is one of the most nerve wracking things a person can do. I'm not sure what it says about me that speaking in public is about the *only* time I'm *relaxed.* Look….I never said I was the boy next door. Here's hopefully a useful tip for speaking in public. Avoid saying "Uh."

Sometimes a speaker says "Uh," so many times, it's all I can remember they said. My suggestion is they just go to silence while they think of their next thought – unless you're on the radio. In public, people are more interested in watching someone think than hearing a lot of "uhs."

The other day I heard a spokesperson for a potential presidential candidate actually say that the potential candidate was announcing that he would be make an announcement. If the following hasn't been said, by *other* potential candidates it's been pretty close.

"I'm forming an exploratory committee to see if I should make an announcement, that I'll be making an announcement." "I'm going on a listening tour to hear what's on the minds of the voters, before I even *think* of making an announcement, that I will be making an announcement." As someone who has never even *dreamed* of making an announcement that I'll be making an announcement – who am I to judge?

Several years ago Senator Torricelli of New Jersey after being severely admonished by the Ethics Committee of the Senate for inappropriately taking gifts, inappropriately using his influence on behalf of the guy, who gave him gifts and a whole lot of other inappropriate things. First he said he agreed with the Ethics Committee's conclusions and fully accepted their findings.

In the next sentence he said "It has always been my contention that I believe that at no time did I accept any gifts." *Then* he said that he had spent long nights "tormented by the question of how I could have allowed such lapses of judgment" which a minute ago he said he believed he never had done. Reading the Senator's statement a sense of dizziness came over me that I haven't experienced since my last ride at an amusement park as a kid on a tilt-a-whirl.

I was pleased years ago, to hear that President Obama had chosen former Senate Majority Leader George Mitchell to be our new Middle East envoy. Senator Mitchell led a team that negotiated the peace treaty in Northern Ireland, a task once seen as impossible to achieve as peace in the Middle East seems now. He also issued a report in 2001 on the escalating violence in the Middle East that was considered impartial by both sides.

He has *another* asset that has not been talked about. I met with Senator Mitchell once to solicit his help in getting rid of an unjust law only America has. As I left, I looked at him and did a joke I've done with bald people and people with very thin hair. I've done this about a hundred times. I look at the person with little hair and jokingly say "You *cannot* tell that is a piece. You see no lace. You see no glue." The Senator was the only person I've ever said that to, who responded "And you see no *hair*." A sense of humor is helpful in any situation.

Years ago I saw some video of legislators in Taiwan leaping across desks, punching each other, wrestling each other to the floor. The whole place was bedlam. I think of that every time I hear a politician say "I will fight for you. I'm a fighter. You can count on me to fight."

Maybe the questions we should ask those running for office should be "What kind of shape are you in? Do you regularly do pushups, sit ups? Can you take a blow to the midsection?" Maybe the politicians should be seen in gyms instead of the campaign trail, in *gyms* training to fight. Just a suggestion.

In nineteen ninety six, I had Jerry Seinfeld as a guest on my cable show. I asked him what he thought of the political campaign. He said he felt it was embarrass-ing. People get up and say elect me as your President and Vice President – *me* to lead the free world. I agreed with Jerry. Gold bless everyone, but I'm not sure I can lead my family. So if you want to lead the free world, bless you. Maybe you're heaven sent or a genius, but personally I wouldn't *dream* of trying to lead the free world.

John Kerry is an authentic American war hero, and yet in the homestretch when he was running for president, he still had to prove he's a regular guy. He's put his life at risk. He's been shot at and *wounded,* and still he has to prove he's a "regular guy."

So he has to go hunting, shoot *birds, anything* to prove he's a regular guy. Watch football. Maybe he'd like to just kick back somewhere and think about policy – work on speeches but no he's got to go out there in the field somewhere shoot a bird, and prove he's a regular guy.

When you're married to just about the richest woman in the world, even if you *are* a war hero – you have to grab a gun, shoot a bird, and prove you're a regular guy. Even some cheeky

[202]

reporter might call out, as one did, "How come you're not *carrying* the bird? "Because I'm lazy" the Senator retorted. Not a bad regular guy retort.

I've never met Senator Kerry, but I once asked Al Gore how he could fly all over the country endlessly talking about and doing this and that – whatever it took to be elected president. He said "I feel strongly about the issues."

Do you really believe Al Gore, John Kerry or George Bush really feel so much stronger about the issues than millions of us other concerned citizens? I don't. I think guys who choose to run for president are a special breed. I'm glad we have them, but I wouldn't want to *be* them, and I *sure* don't want to have to go around shooting birds to prove I'm a regular guy.

Several years ago President Bush's daughters were accused of underage drinking. The Secret Service's mission is to guard the lives of the people they're assigned to. Not that I'm any kind of authority on how exactly you do that, but you'd assume to guard someone, you have to constantly keep an eye on them.

When I was growing up, if my dad decided to go for the presidency I'd sure want him to consider what kind of pressure that was going to put on my teenage activities. It's one thing to be at a party and casually say "Yeah, my dad's running for president," or stand at the podium at the convention, hugging and kissing with balloons falling all around. It's an entirely different can of worms, if you slip out somewhere to do a surreptitious teenage thing and have some guy with a gun peering around a corner at your girl.

Actually President Bush said that in 1998 his daughters asked him *not* to run. They probably knew what they were in for, but decided to try to get away with it anyway. They don't call them teenagers for nothing. An anonymous Secret Service source was quoted as saying, "You can be sure agents have already told the Bush girls they shouldn't be doing this kind of stuff. We do that all the time. Chelsea Clinton listened to her agents. These girls *aren't* listening to their agents."

The Bush girls take a double hit with that quote. They don't listen to their agents and Chelsea did. *That* hurts. At that point they must have felt like if they order a beer, some representative of law enforcement is going to leap out from behind a post, flash a badge and scream "You're under arrest!"

So the girls were causing some embarrassment for their folks. What to do? When Al Gore was Vice President he and Tipper got the Secret Service to back off their seventeen year old, Albert Gore the 3rd one day. That's when *he* was nabbed for speeding 100 m.p.h. on a North Carolina highway.

One of the Bush girls also raced at 100 mph with the Secret Service in pursuit. As I understand it, she was late for a World Wrestling Federation event. She's either an incredible wrestling fan, or could it be that any young person who's constantly being watched might occasionally go a little *nuts*! *I* would. Personally, I would have liked to see my dad walk around getting saluted and applauded all the time, but when I factor in my Secret Service detail, I think my childhood would have been *way* too tense.

Ever since I was old enough to understand anything about government, I've been hearing about advisory staffs. They're all over the place. Things that sound like "The Council of

Economic Advisors," "The National Security Council Advisory Staff," "The President's Advisory Staff on Physical Fitness."

I'm always happy to hear they're there. I like to see our President and our government has as many advisors as possible. I understand that too many cooks can spoil the pot, or whatever that expression is, but on balance I like to see a lot of advisors, even if they *might* spoil the pot.

Particularly in the case of the President, no matter who he or she is, I'm more comfortable if they have more advisors than they can keep track of. I find the concept of one person being the leader of the free world so daunting, that I'm sure for my own personal comfort, I've always imagined that there was an incredibly smart person in the *basement* of the White House, someone that the President could go to – maybe slip down some back stairs to see what *they* thought of *whatever*.

Years ago because I had heard his name around more than one administration; his name was Clark Clifford. He first showed up on the scene in the Truman administration. Since then I hoped Mr. Clifford was down there in the basement somewhere. Then years later I read he was arrested or indicted, or they were *talking* about arresting or indicting him. I don't know what if anything came of all that, but any way you look at it, it wasn't good. He's not around anymore, although in spite of everything I always got the impression he was pretty darn smart. I don't know if we have anyone down there in the basement today, but I sure *hope* we do!

A subject really to be avoided in any social gathering these days is what did you think of the debates? It's just not a fun question. It won't lead to laughs or even smiles, and I don't know...isn't that what social gatherings are kind of supposed to be about?

If you're for one guy, you most likely find him strong, resolute, determined, keeps his eye on the ball – all that good stuff, and you most likely find his opponent wishy-washy, flippy-floppy – all that bad stuff. You find your man thoughtful, intelligent, maybe even visionary, all that good stuff, and you find the other guy bull headed, not that bright, even whiny – all that bad stuff. Have you ever seen a conversation on television, or off television in a living room --

anywhere -- where one person was *persuaded* to the other's point of view?

We're all pretty subjective. It's probably a good idea to be more objective, but when's the last time you saw someone suddenly become more objective? Have you ever heard, "Oh yeah, you're right, the senator is wishy-washy. "Oh yeah, I see the President is an inflexible whiner." If that ever happened, it could make the evening news. That's why when anyone asks me what I think of the debates, I say "Excuse me, may I use your treadmill?"

What if they had an election and no one voted? A city council candidate in Missouri was up for re-election. No one was running against him, and no one came to vote including the city council member, so he kept his seat. Everyone just forgot there was an election. It reminds me of Steve Martin's great line when the tax collector knocked on his door, because he hadn't paid his taxes. He said "I *forgot.*"

Not that we *need* to be reminded, but there's *always* been trouble everywhere. Around 1,000 A.D., the King of England was a fella by the name of Ethelred II, the Unready. I doubt he referred to *himself* as the Unready, but probably so many *others* did, it stuck.

He succeeded to the throne, after the murder of his half-brother, Edward II, the Martyr. He was plagued by poor advice from his personal favorites. He had a rather long and ineffective reign, which was notable for little other than his ongoing attempt to buy off the Danish Viking invaders. Because of the relentless invasions by the Vikings and their demands for *more* money, he abandoned his throne in 1013. He fled to Normandy for safety but was recalled to his throne a year later at the death of Sven Forkbeard. He died two years later. Ethelred the II, the Unready.

A man running for governor and senate in Tennessee tried to be listed only by his middle name which is "None of the above." His middle name was originally Leroy. The would be candidate, David Gatechell argued that other candidates had been allowed to use what he referred to their nicknames on ballots – Walter Combat Ward, Carl Twofeathers Whitaker – they used their full names.

He argued that his middle name "None of the above" was widely known, but he *only* wanted to go with his middle name on the ballot "None of the above." What if I ran for something and I changed my middle name from Sidney which it is to Charles The Greatest American Ever Grodin, but I just wanted to be listed by my middle name The Greatest American Ever. None of the above. I don't *think* so.

The election primary period ended recently, and one aspect of it really fascinated me. Over and over I would see on television or hear on radio ads trumpeting what this or that candidate's plans were for a better America. The problem was I'd never *heard* of most of these people, had *no* idea who they were, *and they didn't tell us. But* they had a *plan*! "I will create more jobs, cut taxes, make America more secure around the world and safer at *home*! Vote for *me*."

Sounds like a plan, but who *are* you? What have you being doing with your life, before you made this ad? An escaped convict could put forth a heck of a plan too, but personally I'd appreciate *knowing* he's an escaped convict. I think, in the future, if the public doesn't know who you are – maybe just *one* sentence to identify yourself in

your ad *besides* your name would be helpful.
Who *are* these people with all these plans?!

For a long time now, I've cringed whenever I
hear a politician use the word, "folks." Has
there ever been a word more designed to have
people like you? "I understand the needs of you
folks out there." Folks. It's...folksie. I think
what makes me cringe about *folks* is it implies a
caring, that is too often contradicted by the
politician's actions that speak *louder* about *lack*
of caring.

We've had too many of the same problems in
America for too long for me to hear "folks."
Mentally ill in prisons *in* America. Hunger *in*
America. Homeless *in* America. *Folks* just
isn't having the effect on me it's designed to.
It's actually having the opposite effect. I find it
alienating. Besides I always thought folks meant
family. I'll buy "My fellow Americans." The
last politician who consistently used that phrase
was elected president four times. I'll *buy* "My
fellow Americans." Just don't give me "folks."

One of the many things that struck me about
former Defense Secretary, Rumsfeld was he
often seemed to be making, what I would call

the non apology apology. The words were there, but the tone too often sounded like this: "It was my fault, *o.k.*?! I should have been on it more, *alright*?! I should have been more aware of the consequences of the photographs and brought it to the President's attention. I *know* that. I've *said* that! *O.k.*?!" Those are my words, but sometimes the Secretary's tone. The non apology apology. Apologies need words *and* tone.

We've never had a shortage of people, who want to be President of the United States. There are many reasons why they *say* they want the office. Usually it's about serving the country etc. etc. I'm *sure* that's true, but there's probably more to it than that.

The job *does* have a lot of perks. Often they play Hail to the Chief, when you come into a room. The crowd stands and applauds. People are always saluting you. *That* could certainly give you a feeling of importance, *although* I could see where it could get pretty *tiring* saluting *back*. One of the really noticeable problems with the job though is once you get it, it doesn't take that long before millions of people start viciously attacking you.

In those increasingly rare times I venture out into the world, I often run into people who say "I really miss seeing you on television." For those of you who may not know, I was on television around seven years or so doing some version of the commentaries I now do on radio.

As I've said, some people even say I wish you'd run for office. I always smile and thank them, and I hope politely, move to another part of the room. Because I don't want to get into a whole thing on the subject; the whole thing would be about how I don't want to be on television. I want to be on the radio – mostly because I can be on radio from home.

As for running for office – same thing. As I've said, you have to constantly ask people for money. You have to go to a heck of a lot of places and stay there a long time, and if you win, you *really* have to go somewhere for long periods, and sit through a lot of long meetings, when you're *not* on the phone asking people for money.

But lately as I look around and see things appear to be falling apart just about everywhere, I'm reconsidering the running for office thing. Duty calls. I'm even thinking of running for president. Don't get me wrong. I don't mean President of the United States. I'm not nuts, or even remotely qualified. Of course, that hasn't stopped some people. No. President of the United States is not for me.

Maybe president of the PTA, because I think our school's curriculum is a mess.   Numerical trigonometry is compulsory. Hellooo?   But the presidency of the PTA would probably involve a lot of meetings, and it probably would take years if ever, before I could knock some of those math and science courses off the curriculum except of course for the aspiring mathematicians and scientists. No, the PTA probably wouldn't work, but I would like to be president of *something*. Is there any way you could be president of something from your house?

It's amazing what you hear if you really listen closely to what some people say. The Mayor of Desert Hot Springs, California, a town that filed for bankruptcy protection, made an interesting statement. The Mayor, who is *also* bankrupt as well, as well as pretty unpopular, wanted to change his term from two years to four. One of his arguments was that it would save the town money to not have an election. But unfortunately for him, a clerk in the county registrar's office discovered it would *not* save the town money. It would *cost* the town twenty five hundred dollars to notify voters of the change. When politicians talk, *if* you're listening – you have to listen *very* carefully.

I have little to no interest in watching these endless presidential debates. The way I see it anyone running for president should have compiled a significant enough record in their other jobs to *justify* running for president. I'm more interested in studying what they've already done rather than what they *say* they're going to do, because *that* always changes, as circumstances change.

But the other day while flipping channels I watched as Fred Thompson said in a debate "The problem with Democrats is they think everyone who works for a living is rich." He seemed serious. It wasn't some kind of a joke. Does he actually believe that? Fred Thompson has spent his life in politics *and* as an actor. Anyone given that line as an *actor* would have to ask who *is* this character I'm playing? Who is Fred Thompson? Who are *any* of these people running? Who has the time to really find out? There are so many of them. As Mel Brooks once wrote; "Hope for the best. Expect the worst."

I have been a news junkie for as long as I can remember. When the 1960 election was in doubt, it was reported Senator Kennedy went to bed around 2:00 a.m. Not me. Like millions, I stayed awake all night to find out who won. While then Governor Bush worked out in a gym, I didn't miss a word of the broadcast of the Supreme Court audio. I was glued to the t.v. set throughout Watergate, Iran Contra and the impeachment of President Clinton.

With Watergate, I was watching when Senator Baker first said, "What did the president know, and when did he know it?" When Oliver North raised his right hand with a chest full of medals, when Admiral Poindexter talked about "plausible deniability" for President Reagan in Iran Contra, I was watching. With the battle over the impeachment, I, of course, was a wall to wall coverage guy.

I was there through the network Florida call for Gore, *then* Bush, then undecided. I was there for the whole pregnant, dimpled chad saga. I followed every minute of every court's proceedings. I was watching when the story moved on to cabinet selections, and will there be Democrats joining the administration? The "Let's all get together for the good of the country" thing seemed to last for about three days, and then suddenly all the hostile bickering where each side portrays itself as completely right and the other as completely wrong caught up with me. Somewhere in there I OD'd on it all.

High drama started to feel like endless too often meaningless drama. I became the Paddy Chayefsky character who cried out something like "I'm mad as hell, and I can't take it anymore." I wasn't really mad, but I sure couldn't take it anymore. For the first time ever, in a major news story, I reached for my remote and changed the channel. I unexpectedly found myself for the longest time just staring at these French cooks with huge white hats, setting sauces on fire. Part of me felt I should switch and check out the latest news, but I stayed with the sauces.

Eventually on some adventure channel, I watched a fella who had lost both legs climb up the steepest mountain I've ever seen. I mean this mountain had absolutely no slant. When he got to the top, he hung upside down for about three minutes and checked out the vista, and I did as well, of course, from my Stratolounger.

I started to watch re-runs of old game shows from the 70's for a while. I have no idea why, but it was kind of relaxing to look at those long sideburns and checkered jackets. I also enjoyed watching people play volleyball on a beach somewhere, and even though I don't understand the language, I began to watch Spanish soap operas.

Then on some animal channel, I watched an incredible confrontation between a huge bear and a lion over a deer carcass. The lion had killed the dear, and the bear came along and looked like he could have taken over the situation, but the lion was snarling so much, the bear eventually decided he wasn't in the mood, and sauntered off. Once I was on the animal channel, it was hard to switch.

I watched people capturing crocodiles for some reason that I couldn't figure out. You had your various large cats stalking gazelles. When they brought them down, I looked away, but I didn't switch, because soon rhinos were charging trucks somewhere.

I'm back watching all the political news again, because I'm the kind of guy who can't bring himself to go through life not knowing who the Secretary of whatever is and what they're up to, but I have learned this. Whenever it all starts to be too much again, and I'm sure it soon will, there's always the animal channel. It's really not that different than watching the latest political news.

One of the oddest things in political ads is hearing the candidate coming on at the end and saying I'm so, and so and I approve this message. I remember former New York City Mayor Ed Koch raving about Congressman Peter King. He ends his ad with "I love the guy," and then we hear the Congressman say "I'm Congressman Peter King and I approve this message." Well, yeah, it's a rave for him. Who wouldn't approve a rave for themselves?

I'm sure this has been going on in previous elections, but for whatever reason I'm more aware of it. The oddest one was Governor Jodi Rell of Connecticut. She came on and talked about her achievements, and then ended by saying "I approve this message." Well yeah! I mean she's the only one talking in the ad. I *assume* she approves of what she just said. What's she going to say I *don't* approve of what I just said? It's a law the candidate has to say that, and I'm sure there's a reason for it – but it just feels strange.

A New York upstate Republican once said that because Senator John Kerry is married to Teresa Heinz, the use of Heinz ketchup is equal to supporting the Democratic nominee for president. The vice president for communications for Heinz said "Heinz ketchup is America's favorite ketchup and is enjoyed by Republicans, Democrats and Independents alike." Nevertheless the upstate Republican said he will not eat one ounce of Heinz ketchup until after Election Day. He'll show *them!*

SPORTS

"In the old days we didn't even have dirt."

Baseball is here again. That's, for me, the good news. The bad news is booing is back. Booing, of course, takes place in all sports. It's just that I watch a lot of baseball on television, so I hear a lot more booing *these* days, and I don't like it. I remember years ago Carlos Beltran, who signed a $119 million dollar multiyear contract with the New York Mets was booed unmercifully last year by some Met fans, when he failed to live up to expectations. It began again this year, when he got off to a slow start.

Then he got very productive, and the booing turned to cheers. After a home run, the fans wanted him to come out of the dugout to take a bow. Carlos really didn't want to, but the manager and an older player urged him to do it, so he did. Carlos said, on reflection, he feels that's what God would have wanted him to do.

Happily, I'm not in any kind of situation where booing is likely. Since I spend most of my work time alone writing, there's really no one around to boo me. Socially I've never gotten booed, although I have to admit on more than one occasion I've felt the possibility in the air. Personally, *I* would not take a bow, if you cheered me after you booed me, which would no question provoke more booing. I see myself as very fortunate I don't work in large stadiums.

When a former major league baseball commissioner passed away, a strange story emerged about his selection to be the sports chief executive. It seems the owners on the committee given the job to recruit him had gotten the wrong man.

There were two retired military men with similar names. One was a baseball expert and the other...well, he liked baseball. The selection committee recruited the guy who liked baseball, and after a few years on the job the mistake was evident, and the commissioner moved on.

I always get a smile when I'm listening to a baseball game – there can be a tense situation, a commercial will come on and the announcer will say "If you have a serious medical condition, contact such and such hospital." Thankfully I don't *have* a serious medical condition, although sometimes in some tense sports situation, I feel like one might be coming on. Hey, maybe that's why they give you the hospital commercial at those times! I never thought of that.

I'm always fascinated when a baseball manager races out of the dugout and argues with an umpire about some decision that didn't go his team's way. The umpire is right where the play happened, and the manager is sitting off in a dugout. That doesn't mean the umpire's always right, but who wants to argue with a guy three feet from the event, when you're a hundred feet or more away?

Not me, but they race out there and yell into each other's face for longer than I can believe, before the umpire throws the manager out. I think it's show business. It's good show business too. It holds my attention better than a lot of actual show business stuff. I appreciate it. It actually gets my mind off my problems for a *moment*.

This comes under the heading of "They really think of everything." A friend of mine called me the other day to say he had shot a hole in one at some club. He then had a responsibility to buy everyone at the club a drink. When I told

another friend the story he said at *his* club you
can buy hole-in-one insurance, so the insurance
company pays for the drinks in the event you get
a hole in one. Personally, I think dealing with an
insurance company would take the fun out of the
hole in one.

I found it funny once when I was watching a
New York Met baseball game and the announcer
Ted Robinson said that playing first base was a
more *social* position than catching. He was
talking about Met catcher Mike Piazza, who was
playing some first base that year.

The announcer said when you're crouching
behind a batter with a mask on, it's harder to
have a little social exchange, than if you're
playing first *without* a mask, of course, and you
can chat with a base runner. The social
opportunities in any field are important.

Years ago because of a rain out on the previous
night, I was watching a rare double header
baseball game on television. When I was a kid,
double headers were regularly scheduled on
Sundays. Now they are a thing of the past. The
announcers were incessantly complaining. They
couldn't believe they were in such a dire work

situation. They kept referring to how many fans had left the park early into the second game. They referred to another game taking place in Philadelphia that had gone into the twelfth inning, and said "Well at least they don't have to play a second game."

The whole thing made *me* feel like one of those guys from another time, who are always talking about what it was like "way back when." "We had to do this, and we had to do that...today, you young people don't realize and on and on."

As I recall fifty years ago in America some things *were* harder, but *some* things were easier. For example it's not a given today as it used to be that somebody who has a full time job can support a family. My favorite line though from somebody who wants to point out how tough it used to be is "In the old days, we didn't even have *dirt*."

Baseball's winter meetings ended recently, and there have been a number of big ticket signings. The guy signs for 32 million for three years. That guy signs for 45 million for four years. 50 million for this long. 60 million for that long.

Not that long ago Alex Rodriquez signed for around 250 million more or less – actually more.

I'm positive I'm not the only would be former athlete who has stopped and asked myself "What if?" I was an aspiring baseball pitcher as a teen. I had no velocity, but I did have location, meaning I was very good at having the ball go where I wanted it to, and on a curve as well.

I *had* location. I once had a conversation with a major league pitcher, and I told him I didn't have velocity but I *did* have location, and he said "Location is everything." So sometimes when I hear about these fifty million dollar contracts, I think to myself "Maybe if…" Naah!

Even though I've been an avid baseball fan all my life I heard one the other day that really startled me. Did you know, in New York anyway, hitters on the New York Mets get to pick what music accompanies them, as they walk toward the batter's box? There was a big outcry in New York years ago when a newly acquired Met pitcher used the same music that the star Yankee pitcher had when he took the mound.

Do *you* have a certain song that's played when you show up for work? Would you like one? What if more than one employee showed up at the same time?

Maybe each employee gets a day to select their special song. I wonder how many songs there are that express the sentiment "Let me out of here?" How would the boss feel about that? Maybe the boss wants a let me out of here song. Maybe couples who aren't speaking could use songs to express their feelings. The possibilities are endless. Less talk – more music.

The Supreme Court has ruled that prayers led by students at athletic events are illegal. The court said they had the effect of coercing others into worship, violating the constitution's ban on state promotion of religion.

So a group called No Pray, No Play sent e-mail messages around Texas encouraging people to come to Santa Fe to pray at a high school football game. The high school, in response, had more than two dozen fire trucks and ambulances on hand in preparation for an anticipated overwhelming crowd of praying protesters. In fact, a much smaller crowd showed up for the game than usual.

Gary Causey, the high school principal said "I think a lot of locals stayed home, because they didn't want to deal with a mess." Outside the football field a group of about two dozen people sang hymns, two men carried wooden crosses, while inside many fans quietly recited the Lord's prayer before the start of the game, but most of the sound came from cheers, clapping hands and shouts for the young players.

Nonetheless Candy Gerulis, a forty three year old hair stylist from Santa Fe who was raised Catholic said to the New York Times; "This is crazy. It makes me feel uncomfortable to have people stand up and start praying around me at a football game."

To me, as someone who too many times has been at sporting events in the middle of a lot of people – who were drunk and screaming obscenities, I wouldn't have a problem with prayers and hymns. Come to think of it, while I understand the importance of separation of church and state, if I could ban *one* thing at games it wouldn't be prayers; it would be loud, mean, drunks.

There was an interesting article in the New York Times about the Toronto Blue Jays general manager J.P. Ricciardi. On his weekly radio show he admitted he lied about the reason one of his pitchers wasn't pitching. He said the pitcher had a sore back. Then more recently the team announced he would have season ending *elbow* surgery.

The general manager then said, "There're a lot of things we don't tell the media, because the media doesn't need to know it, and the fans don't need to know it. They're not lies, if we know the truth." "They're not lies, if we know the truth?!"

Isn't that what a lie is? Deliberately not telling the truth? I always like to get as many sources as I can for what I say, so I checked Webster's dictionary. They define a lie as "an untrue statement made with intent to deceive." I *like* to give the benefit of the doubt. Maybe the general manager doesn't have a dictionary – or *want one.*

Someone connected to the New York Yankees once ran a clip of Al Pacino from the football movie, *Any Given Sunday* giving a pep talk. I assume it was for the players. There's maybe something here we should think about. You want to have a sit down with your kids over some problem?

I'm sure some screen writers and actors have many of those on film. Any difficult situation that you rather not deal with *must* be on film somewhere. The words would be carefully thought out and delivered professionally. Maybe you wouldn't even have to be there. Just leave the clip and hope for the best. Pep talks for the Yankees from Al Pacino on film, opens up limitless possibilities of how to deal with life's problems.

One of the strangest things I ever see when I'm watching baseball on television is a player hits a home run and the pitcher hits the next batter with a pitch as though to retaliate – for *what*?! If he's going to be mad, why not be mad at himself? It's a lot like life. So often things don't go the way someone wants, and they're so quick to be mad at someone other than themselves.

If things don't go your way first look at yourself, then if you're *sure* it's not you *then* look at someone else -- but whatever you do, don't throw a baseball at them.

Years ago the St. Louis Cardinals pitcher Julian Tavarez and the New York Yankee's pitcher Kevin Brown after unsuccessful outings both broke their hands by punching something in their respective dugouts.

They're both right handed pitchers who broke their *left* hands, so they weren't *entirely* out of control. What should a highly competitive person do when he's overcome with frustration? Punch a wall? No. How about just jump up and down and swing your arms in the air? It's not the most macho move, but it definitely won't break any bones, and its good exercise. Just a suggestion.

STUDIES

"I'm surprised I can still be surprised."

I bought a new bathroom scale the other day, because the old one said I weighed eighty pounds. It was a hundred pounds off. When I took my new scale out of the box, there was a survey inside the manufacturer wanted me to fill out.

Here are some of the questions: Who bought the scale? Why did you buy the scale? Where do you intend to use the scale? O.k. reasonable questions. I'm not going to answer them, but reasonable. Then, just because I bought their scale, they wanted to know my education, my birth date and marital status among several more questions. Oh yeah, they also wanted to know my income. I can tell you this; if every time I bought something, I answered all these questions I'd have very little time to earn *any* income.

I saw a study that said we blink ten million times a year. How did they come up with this? Was someone assigned to watch a person every single moment over a year and keep count? What about when the blinker was in the bathroom or shower? What if the blinker woke up when he or she was sleeping and blinked a couple of times before going back to sleep? Was the counter lying next to them in bed? What if the blinker was sleeping with someone? Wouldn't that be a little awkward?

And what if *you* were the blinker? Wouldn't it get on your nerves to have someone *constantly* staring at you every second for a year? We blink ten million times a year? I'm not saying we *don't*, but I'm not buying we do. And everyone blinks the same amount of time? And besides who *cares*?

I was reading an article recently that said according to a study in Michigan older Americans are *happier* than younger Americans. The study polled 542 people on line and asked them about their level of happiness. On a scale of 1-10 with ten representing the highest level of happiness, the younger group reported an average happiness level of 6.65 while the older group reported a level of happiness that was 7.32. Uh huh.

What's your level of happiness? Boy that's a tough one. It would depend on what day and what time of day or even what's the weather like or whether you're asking optimists or pessimists. Level of happiness for people over fifty 7.32? That's .67 higher than for people under fifty. Ah surveys!

First how often do we blink? What should we do about Liberia? The latest is people on juries who have recently showered or even just washed their hands will judge differently. *Really*?!

You mean if a lifelong bigot or racist recently washed their hands, they *won't* judge like a bigot or a racist?! I'd like to see a report on whose money is used to pay for these insightful and terribly important surveys. I just heard a report that they're selling a watch that *doesn't* tell the time. I'm surprised I can still be surprised.

A recent study reported that there are fewer kinds of fish in the ocean. They can tell by observing the different kinds of fish that are caught in those huge fishing nets. There're a lot of explanations for this. Some or maybe *none* are true. One possible explanation I *haven't* heard is there really *aren't* fewer kinds of fish. It's just that the smarter fish *have* learned to avoid the nets.

The New England Journal of Medicine has published a study that says hanging out with a fat person can make you fat too. The study says a person's likelihood of getting pudgy rises by 57%, if he or she has a friend, who is overweight. That risk triples if it's a *close* friend.

If I follow that it means, if you have a pudgy close friend it's 171% likely you'll get pudgy? One of the concerns is a mother may stop her child from playing with an overweight friend. I can imagine *another* scenario. A man or woman meets someone whom they are not particularly attracted to, *but* they're thin. So compatibility, disposition, attraction are out – *thin* is *really* in.

How would you like to be a census taker in Russia? An article in U.S. News and World Report by Masha Gessen says that it's a tough job, because Russia is a country where people *really* don't want to answer questions. They have reason to believe that anything they say can be used against them, so how much do you think they want to tell you? Name and address? Maybe. Stalin banned the publication of a census in the 30's, because it showed the majority of people living in the atheist country believed in God.

Sometimes I like to turn the sound off on the television and just watch the news crawl at the bottom of the screen. I did this the other day while watching CNN, and at one point across the screen, it said "Americans sad three times a month." Where do they come up with this stuff?! It didn't say who *said* Americans are sad three times a month, just that Americans *were* sad.

It didn't say *what* Americans. It didn't say on *average*. It just said Americans are sad three times a month. How many times a month are you sad? Who knows? There's sad and then there's *sad*. You can be sad you can't find a parking place or sad when someone dies, but it just said Americans are sad three times a month. *Okaay.*

A new survey says people form snap judgments of us sometimes in as little time as one twentieth of a second. First of all I don't believe it. Of course, I don't even believe what *experts* say for the most part, let alone these surveys that keep popping up constantly, but if it were true that judgments were made on us in one twentieth of a second, what kind of pressure is *that*? Boy you'd *always* have to have just the right look on your face, the right shirt etc. etc. Oh brother! Naah! I don't believe it.

I saw an interesting piece in the New York Times once about a General Social Survey that's taken every other year, where approximately 3,000 Americans are interviewed for ninety minutes and asked about four hundred fifty questions. Here is some information that particularly interested me. This data is listed from 1972 to 2006. Our trust in others is at a *low* point. For some reason in 1984 it was at a *high* point. I'm sure.

A recent study at Duke University said the brain may use sleep time to consolidate memories made during the day. "*May* use sleep time to consolidate memories."

I guess if it may, it also may *not*. Look I'd like to understand as much as possible about how everything works, and admittedly maybe I just don't get it, but aren't some things *beyond* knowing, and what does "consolidate memories" mean anyway?

[239]

I would imagine that major corporations wouldn't do things that would reflect badly on them. Anyone with a reasonable amount of common sense could see that having a recording call people *early in the morning* to conduct a survey is *not* a good idea.

Some people work nights, but leave their phones on in case of an emergency. Maybe the first question the recording should ask is "Did I wake you?" The second question could be "Do you resent this call?" If the recording gets two positive yeses and then a hang up – maybe they'll think differently about *early morning surveys*.

Just when I thought it would be harder to get sillier with a survey question – a new one comes along that had me staring into space. I read a Harris Poll claiming Republicans prefer chocolate ice cream, and Democrats prefer vanilla. Okaay.

I found a recent poll conducted by USA Today interesting. The question was "Are public cell phone conversations rude?" I, of course, think they are, and according to the poll 51% of the people asked agreed with me. 37% thought they weren't rude, and 12% weren't sure.

I would guess the 49% who thought they weren't rude or weren't sure are the ones who have public cell phone conversations on trains, buses, etc. All knowing is one of my least favorite things, but I'm sorry; they're rude.

Recently there was a survey that said that *12%* of pet owners call home daily to speak to their pets. "Hi! Put Princess on. What do you mean she's sleeping!? Tell her I'm on the phone!"

Another recent survey revealed that 46% of pet owners have sent a *greeting* card from their dog or cat. 52% of pet owners believe their pet listens to them best. 59% celebrate their pets' birthday. 90% of pet owners would not consider dating someone, who was not fond of their pet. 68% of pet owners travel with their pet.

The survey showed that fireworks upset pets more than anything. People mostly acquire pets for companionship. What a shock! 39% of pet owners found it easy to name their pet.

Then there was the study that revealed that animals have emotions. Have you *ever* seen *any* animal that didn't have emotions? O.K., maybe a cow is a little on the laid back side, but don't worry about it, *cows* have emotions.

There was a study that said if you are distracted while driving your car you are more likely to get into an accident. No kidding! The study *revealed* that if you're texting or looking at your car phone or CD player and not at the road while driving – it's not a good idea.

They had statistics to prove it too. Are there really people out there who didn't *know* if you look away from the road while driving, it's not good? That's a scary thought. Maybe they should do a survey on *that*.

How many people don't *know* if you look away from the road, while driving it's not a good thing? If the number is *high, I'm* taking the train. Some of these surveys are paid for by the government. Since we're always looking for ways to cut back on spending, I suggest we start with some of these surveys.

I was watching Lou Dobbs the other night. He was giving the results of a poll where the question was "Do you believe the stock market would have gone down even more *without* the federal bailout?" What? Who's being asked? Professional economists don't agree. You're asking *us*, the general public? Give me a break!

I heard on the news the other day how many birds were counted in Central Park this year. They gave the number of birds that were counted last year and the year before and the year before that. The numbers are six thousand and higher. *What?*

You think you can count thousands of birds. Years ago they couldn't count, who got the most votes for the Senate in Minnesota, Norm Coleman or Al Franken. That's only two people not thousands of birds flying around a park. Tell me something I can believe, and besides knowing how many birds there are in Central Park is not something at the top of my list of things I need to know.

UNUSUAL PEOPLE

"I don't really get the naked on the floor thing."

I had a conversation recently with a highly successful man who barely spoke above a whisper. He wasn't ill or elderly, and you felt if he wanted to, he could easily speak at a normal volume. I mean he was from Texas, and Texans aren't particularly known for whispering. I haven't met anyone like that in over thirty years, when I remember meeting with another highly successful man, who also barely spoke above a whisper.

In this case I *also* had the feeling he was perfectly able to speak at a normal volume. Whether this was conscious or unconscious, and I believe at some point it *had* to be a conscious choice – it's a power play. You have to lean in and concentrate like crazy to hear them. In hindsight, I think I resent this. The next time someone pulls that whispering power play on me, I'm going to say "Would you speak a little louder please?" and I'm sure they will. Ironically, the last thing anyone pulling that kind of power play wants is *not* to be heard.

There was a photograph in the newspaper of the disgraced former head of the International Monetary Fund, Dominique Strauss-Kahn, who appears to be a sex addict. There are less polite terms, but that's bad enough. The photograph showed him with President and Mrs. Obama.

He was leering at Mrs. Obama about to approach her, and if you look closely, you can see the President had his hand on him to hold him back. If he hadn't and Strauss-Kahn made one of his absurd sexual moves, I would have liked to have seen Mrs. Obama smack him across the face. That would be a smack heard and cheered around the world.

I have what some might see as a flaw, but I see as an asset. I don't assume, because someone is in a position of authority that they are necessarily more knowledgeable or more anything on the positive side than someone else.

This came to mind recently when I read of the fourth grade teacher in upstate *New York* who made one of his nine year old students wear his New York Yankee tee shirt inside out. The teacher has Boston Red Sox paraphernalia all over his classroom. And this man is a *teacher*?!

Years ago Robert John Burch, who was better known around New York City as "The Naked Cowboy" would stand on a street corner in Times Square and plays the guitar dressed only in his cowboy boots and jockey shorts. He was very muscular, and until he started appearing in his underpants he hadn't garnered much attention.

His mission statement is "I will dominate the world's markets through the commercialization of the greatest product service ever created – me. I think I am God. I totally believe in myself." He's been arrested more than forty times, but somehow he's legal in his undies at Time Square, where he says he makes close to a thousand a day in tips. There *is* no business like show business. Later he withdrew as a candidate for mayor of New York.

I was having lunch the other day with Barry Levinson. Barry Levinson is one of the greatest American film directors. He directed among countless others Rain Man with Dustin Hoffman and Tom Cruise for which he won the Academy Award as best director. Barry Levinson is a smart guy. Even though it was the first time I've ever met him, it's obvious Barry is a very smart guy, and Barry asked, I'm sure rhetorically, because he couldn't have expected me to answer, "How is it man came up with the wheel *many* centuries before man came up with the sandwich?"

Barry said man figured out how to make and use a wheel to haul things etc. *centuries* before anyone sitting somewhere said "Y'know there's two slices of bread over there – there's some meat – let's put that meat between that bread – hence what we now know as a sandwich." Much simpler concept than the *wheel* you'd have to say, and yet the sandwich came *centuries* after the wheel.

When you think about it, that's probably because necessity is the mother of invention, and no doubt we need wheels more than we need sandwiches – no disrespect to sandwiches. The sandwich is called a sandwich, because it was named after the Earl of Sandwich. The reason the sandwich was named after the Earl, was because the Earl wanted to *eat* while he was at the gambling table, so he ate food in that form while gambling and someone, I guess who had the authority to do it, named the sandwich after him.

Before that, I assume the sandwich didn't even *have* a name. There's no Earl of the Wheel, because that happened so long ago they weren't even thinking of titles or giving credit. Credit all this to Barry Levinson.

I really enjoyed a story I read years ago in the New York Times about the last civilian manning a light house in the United States. He's eighty five years old. His name is Frank Schubert, and he really would just like to be left alone!

He has been tending lighthouses since 1937, when he joined the Coast Guard as a civilian and has been manning the lighthouse at Coney Island since 1960. A national radio program found him, interviewed him and now all kinds of people want to talk to him!

Mr. Schubert says "My head's going to explode. I don't have anything interesting to tell." His bosses at the Coast Guard say it's good publicity, but Mr. Schubert wonders "What does the Coast Guard need with publicity? Who doesn't know who the hell the Coast Guard is?"

[250]

According to the Times, Mr. Schubert says "People think there's something romantic about a lighthouse. It's just a *lighthouse!* Yeah, yeah, yeah, I'm the last civilian manning a lighthouse. *So what!"*

It's a refreshing story at a time when so many people seem to be knocking each other over for 15 minutes of fame. Maybe they should get a job at a lighthouse.

In the category of "You've got to be kidding," a man in Germany went to the police to complain that a bag of marijuana he had paid $475.00 for really wasn't up to his standards. "Unusable," he said.

 He tried first going to his dealer but got no satisfaction there, which caused him to file a complaint with the police, who instead filed a complaint against him for violating the drug possession law.   Sounds like he already smoked too much.

I was a guest speaker at a charity event recently. I had my picture taken with what seemed like all three hundred and fifty people who attended.

One guy in particular got my attention, because instead of saying the usual "Hello" or "Nice to meet you" he said "Congratulations." I wasn't sure for what he was congratulating me. I guess for being the guest speaker.

Later I passed him coming out of the men's room, as I was going in, and he said "Have a good one," and told me some anecdote I can't remember. I wondered what this guy was like around the house. When I was seated waiting to speak, a fellow sitting at the same table I was, held up a photo of me in the program that was taken around 12 years ago. He looked at me with a quizzical expression; I guess it meant I looked 12 years older now than the photo.

I found it all kind of funny. My motto is "If it's not life threatening – look for the humor." Thankfully I haven't had to come up with a motto, if it *is* life threatening. Mottos don't exactly grow on trees.

We know all about the so-called frivolous law suits. The debate is really about what's frivolous and what's not frivolous. Like most of you I'm sure, people suing McDonalds, because they ate so many big Macs they weigh four hundred pounds don't get a lot of my sympathy.

Oh I feel bad for them, because four hundred pounds is a lot of pounds, but not much sympathy in blaming McDonalds for the four hundred. "Hey! Fries are fattening!" That doesn't qualify as news breaking.

Now a guy is suing some casino in Vegas for gambling losses in the millions, because he kept getting extended credit. At first that seemed frivolous, but a second look makes me wonder about the casinos *and* McDonalds.

Is it illegal or un American to say to a four hundred pounder ordering say -- extra fries, "Sorry sir, we're all out, or to a guy who already owes a million to a casino "Why don't you sleep on this a while?" It probably *is* illegal *and* un-American, but I wonder. Personally, of course, I wouldn't want to be there when you tell the fat guy he can't have the fries.

A salute to my brother, big Jack Grodin in Pittsburgh for calling my attention to all the unfriendliness going on at the Friendly

[253]

Restaurant chain. S. Priestly Blake, the co-founder of Friendly, brought a law suit seeking to make the current chairman of Friendly, Donald N. Smith repay part of the cost of operating an eight million dollar jet he used to fly across America. Mr. Blake claims Mr. Smith made personal use of the jet.

The ninety one year old founder also claims other improprieties. Mr. Blake founded Friendly with his brother during the depression with $547 they borrowed from their parents. Mr. Smith, the current Chairman, acknowledges he only works part time, so his alleged personal use of the corporate jet particularly rankles Mr. Blake, who had to sell sixteen of his twenty four Rolls Royces to help finance the law suit. Friendly? What's in a name?

My closest friend when I was twelve was a bright, friendly boy who was also about the clumsiest fella I've ever met. One evening a group of us were sitting in another friend's house having Cokes in the kitchen. My clumsy friend said "Why are we sitting in the kitchen? Why don't we go sit in the living room, where it's more comfortable?" Our host said his parents preferred we hang out in the kitchen, and besides he said our clumsy friend probably would spill his Coke the minute we entered the living room.

On hearing that, my clumsy friend really was insulted, and *insisted* we stop this nonsense and head into the living room immediately, which we did. The minute my friend entered the living room he tripped and spilled his Coke.

I was watching a fishing show the other day where the host was fishing with a man 100 years old. The host asked the man if he had anything he'd like to pass on to us. The 100 year old man said most people look at him and assume he doesn't know what he's doing, and then when he does something, people assume he can do *more* than he actually can which is, of course, the Peter principle.

People who can do something keep getting promoted and too often wind up in a job they're not really qualified for. Clearly we don't have to wait until someone's 100 to see that happen.

This is for anyone out there who may actually believe what it says on some magazine covers. One that recently caught my eye was a photo of the singer /actress Vanessa Williams who is quoted as saying "At 44 I know who I am and I'm enjoying every moment."

I don't know Vanessa Williams, and maybe she *does* know who she is, and enjoys every moment?! As far as I know Jack Nicholson hasn't been quoted as saying *he* enjoys every moment, but every photo I see of him he's grinning from ear to ear as *though* he is enjoying every moment.

I know Jack Nicholson. I like Jack Nicholson. Jack Nicholson has a magnificent career, but not even Jack Nicholson enjoys *every* moment. Vanessa and Jack – enjoy *a lot* of moments – maybe – but *every* moment? Naah!

I was sorry to read that former Los Angeles Dodger manager Tommy LaSorda suffered a mild heart attack. He ended his managerial career in 1996 after suffering a heart attack. Of course, I wish him the best. I know Tommy. He once said something I found memorably funny. I introduced him to my wife years ago. He shook her hand and said "My condolences."

A Nobel Prize winning author recently said that "Female writers have a narrow view of the world. They are unequal to me." He also said a woman is not a complete master of her house, so that comes over in her writing.

I don't know whose house he's *talking* about. He also said he didn't mean any of this in an unkind way. I would say to him, *you don't know what you're talking about*! Of course, I don't mean that in an unkind way.

When the reclusive author of *The Catcher in the Rye*, J.D. Salinger died his obituary said he had spent most of his adult life keeping himself isolated from just about everyone. No one can say exactly *why* he chose to do that, but it was widely reported that he just didn't want to deal with the day to day nonsense that most of us deal with.

It reminds me of a story a friend of mine told me. He was auditioning for a movie to be filmed in Toronto. His audition floored everyone. They were so excited, that as he left they called after him "See you in Toronto." He never heard from them again.

My experience in this vein happened about twenty five years ago. I read aloud a movie I had written to this couple who financed movies. When I finished they said "We're going to make your movie."

A couple of weeks later I heard they weren't. I called the man of the couple and said "I thought you were going to make my movie?" He said "When we say we're going to make your movie, that doesn't mean we're going to make your movie." He said some things after that, but I don't' remember what they were. We all in a way can identify with the wish of J.D. Salinger to be out of touch.

For some reason I've been blessed to always be wary of authority especially, if it's presented as the *ultimate* authority. I ran into this when I was a young acting student, and a widely celebrated speech teacher came to our class. She listened to me recite something for a couple of minutes and proceeded to rip me apart, because of my quote "Poor speech."

She asked how I could possibly expect anyone to pay to see me perform when I spoke the way I did - which is by the way how I speak now. She was asking for what she called mid-Atlantic speech, but it seemed to me she was asking me to speak with an English accent.

If I had followed her advice, I don't believe I would ever have made a living as an actor in America – in England *maybe*. Beware of these all-knowing authorities.

It seems as though every day Donald Trump is into it with someone else. This time it's Robert DeNiro. DeNiro had said certain people in the news are making statements about people that they don't back up. He was talking about Donald Trump's questioning if President Obama was born in America.

Trump fired back "I like DeNiro's acting, but we're not dealing with Albert Einstein. He's not the brightest bulb on the planet." I've known Donald Trump and Robert DeNiro for several years. Both have built empires.

Unlike Trump, DeNiro has never had to file for bankruptcy protection. Most importantly, I've never known Bob DeNiro to have alienated anyone. Donald Trump? The list is too long to count. Personally, I'd be more comfortable with Robert DeNiro as president than Donald Trump.

I know some very bright people, who have surprisingly holes in what they know. I'm not going to call myself very bright, but my I.Q. *is* in triple digits. I think I knew, before my wife confirmed it that the sun rises in the East and sets in the West, but if you asked me to quickly point out to you, which way is East, West, North or South, I wouldn't want to bet on my ability to do it.

I believe the brain has a left lobe and a right one and probably one up front as well, but I wouldn't swear I know the left and right lobe's function. This – even though I've actually been the voice of one of the lobes at Epcot Center at Disneyworld for several years.

I once had an exchange with a friend many years ago, who was comparing Barbra Streisand's lobes with mine. I don't even remember exactly what was said except it was about Barbra's and my lobes. According to my friend, she had a more developed left or right lobe than I did, and I had the better…other lobe. My point is no matter to whom you're speaking, don't assume they know more than you know. Of course, don't assume they *don't* either.

More and more I see people wearing little pieces of jewelry in their ears, above their eyes on their nose and *on their lips*. To each his own, but the other day I saw a mother wearing her rings on her lips and she was carrying a small baby. *Hellooo*. There should be a law. No lip rings, if you have a little one.

Years ago when Senator Bob Graham was running for the Democratic nomination for president, it was reported he kept a personal log of his day from the time he wakes up, until he goes to bed. That included everything from what times he eats, practices golf, plays golf, what time he returned the golf cart, and what time he was in the bathroom.

This all came to mind, when it was reported that Senator Jon Tester of Montana, when he travels takes with him a forty pound roller bag, which he stuffs into the overhead bin of the airplane. It is filled with *meat* – roasts, ribs, round steak, rib steak.

The Senator explained "We like our own meat."
Well…obviously if someone holds political
office or is running for it – they're clearly not
the boy or girl next door. I wonder if Senator
Tester keeps track of the *time* he eats the meat he
flies with.

My longtime friend, Ria Berkus told me a good
one the other day. She said "You start out
believing in Santa. Then you *don't* believe in
Santa. Then you *become* Santa. *Then* you *look*
like Santa."

In reading an article by Kirk Johnson in the New
York Times recently, I learned that there are
some people in Boulder, Colorado who have an
interesting take on things. Aren't there
everywhere! Seth Brigham, forty five years old
proudly took off his pants before stepping up to
speak in his shorts at a City Council meeting.
He was speaking out against what he felt was a
growing police crackdown on public nudity.

Each year in Boulder runners take part in the
Naked Pumpkin Run – wearing jack-o-lanterns
on their heads as they run down the street on
Halloween naked. They also have a naked bike
ride. The naked pumpkin run and the naked bike

[262]

ride are the two *biggest* naked events in Boulder. I take from the article that they have some *smaller* naked events.   To each his own.

Years ago I was reading the obituary of Aaron Spelling. Mr. Spelling was the most prolific producer in American television. He produced *Mod Squad, Charlie's Angels, The Love Boat, Dynasty* and *Beverly Hills 90210* among countless others.

What struck me more than anything about Mr. Spelling was he and his wife Candy built a mansion for themselves in the Holmby Hills section of Los Angeles that had one hundred and twenty three rooms. One hundred and twenty three rooms?! This is a *house* not a hotel.

I'm sure he had live in staff, but still, can you imagine coming home and wondering if anyone else was home? You couldn't go around and knock on one hundred and twenty three doors, you'd be exhausted. I assume there must have been plenty of stairs to climb or were there just elevators or escalators?

I have fond feelings for Mr. Spelling, because I was on one of his shows in the sixties, and he said some nice things about me. People being supportive in show business or *any* business are so rare, that as far as I'm concerned Mr. Spelling could have all the rooms he wanted. When he passed away, his wife sold the house. She said "A hundred and twenty six are too many rooms for one person."

It's not a breaking news story that people are different, but as someone who as I've said wears thermal long johns *indoors*, I was startled to read that a growing number of people, overwhelmingly men, like to hike in the *nude* on the snow covered Swiss alps – in the *snow* – in the *nude*.

It's reported in the New York Times there's a danger of sunburn, of course, but also of ticks carrying Lyme disease. Then there's always freezing to death. People really *are* different.

A federal appeals court cleared the way for an artist to photograph a large group of naked people on a street in lower Manhattan. The court ruled that the time for the photograph be chosen when it would cause "a minimal intrusion on the neighborhood." In other words; probably not at rush hour.

[264]

The photographer, Spencer Tunick, is known for taking photographs of naked people in public. In the past he has photographed naked people in Central Park and on city streets and bridges. Mr. Tunick has been arrested five times in New York, although all the charges have been dropped.

Last year he was arrested while trying to photograph a group of naked people in Times Square. He has recently sued the City to stop them from arresting him, as he plans to photograph a group of sunburned naked people beneath a large picture of a lobster in lower Manhattan.

His attorney, Ron Kuby argued that he should be allowed to do this based on his right to "artistic expression." In a 2-1 decision, the court ruled that Mr. Tunick be allowed to photograph the naked people. The attorney Mr. Kuby now says his client plans to take a different photograph. Instead of the sunburned naked people under the lobster, Mr. Tunick plans to photograph naked people under the Williamsburg bridge. So if you're driving over that bridge, for safety's sake, *please* keep your eyes on the road.

[265]

There was a photograph taken of four hundred fifty naked women on the floor of Grand Central terminal recently. I assume they closed the terminal for this. The picture was taken at 3:00 a.m. I saw the photo in the New York Post. The women are supposed to be in formations to imitate streets, buildings and cityscapes.

I don't know…to me it just looks like a lot of naked women lying on the floor. The photographer said he wanted to bring the most beautiful people into the city's most beautiful building. I wonder if he ever thought of just throwing a big *party* and inviting a lot of beautiful people – dressed. I don't really get the naked on the floor thing.

According to an article in the N.Y. Times, Edward Bello, who is sixty years old has been arrested many times over the last thirty years and been found guilty several times but has never spent a day in jail. He recently pleaded guilty in New York City to having stolen credit cards with, of course, the intent to use them. Still no jail. The judge sentenced him to ten months of home detention, *but* he's not allowed to watch t.v.!

His lawyers, not satisfied that Mr. Bello *still* wasn't going to jail, are challenging the no t.v. order. They claim *that* punishment violates Mr. Bello's first amendment rights. The first amendment guarantees freedom of religion, speech and the right to assemble, nothing about watching t.v. in there.

One attorney felt they might more logically argue an eighth amendment violation – cruel and unusual punishment. The judge felt that Mr. Bello had "skirted the edges of criminal behavior for too long." I don't know …stealing someone's credit card is skirting the *edges* of criminal behavior. Feels more like the *center* to me.

Mr. Bello, who lives with his wife and daughters, who are thirteen and fourteen years old has seven television sets. His lawyer persuaded the judge that his daughters be allowed to keep their t.v. sets in their rooms, but only for the girls and their mothers to watch. Mr. Bello gave his *word* that he won't watch.

If he breaks his word, I can hear the call now. "Judge, I just saw my dad watching t.v., you better come take him to jail." But that can't happen for a while though, because Mr. Bello's attorneys got an appellate court to delay the t.v. ban, while they prepare their appeal, so Mr. Bello is home watching television, even though he has been arrested over and over for thirty years and recently stole someone's credit card. If he loses his appeal, for ten months he will actually have to stop watching t.v. at home. That's some system – our justice system.

This comes under the heading of some questions are better left not asked. A man in Bosnia faked his own death, because he wanted to see how many people would show up at his funeral. He hid in nearby bushes to watch. Turns out only one person showed up – his mom.

He was furious and sent an angry letter to forty five people saying he paid a lot of money to get a fake death certificate and bribed undertakers to deliver an empty coffin. He said "I really thought a lot more of you, my so-called friends, would turn up to pay their last respects." There's so much wrong with this man's judgment, I don't know where to begin.

First of all, if you're sitting around wondering how many of your friends would come to your funeral – well…that's a heck of a thing to be sitting around wondering about. Kind of suggests *you* be nicer to your friends.

Sir John Gielgud was considered the last of the three greatest English actors of the past fifty years. Sir Lawrence Olivier and Sir Ralph Richardson were the other two. I saw John Gielgud and Ralph Richardson in a play called *No Man's Land* about twenty five years ago on a Friday night and was back the next afternoon to watch the Saturday matinee.

A year earlier I had worked with John Gielgud in a movie in London, and I was struck by his grace and humility. When I was first introduced to him, before I could say a word, he complimented me on an earlier movie I'd done.

Once I asked him to come with me to watch the film of the previous day's work at lunch and he said he hadn't been invited. When I told him I was sure it would be fine, he reluctantly came along. As soon as he saw the director, a man like considerably less accomplished than Sir John, he said to him. "Oh is it alright, Chuck invited me to come along." Of course, it was.

I was talking about all of this with a friend of mine, and he told me he had once been invited to observe John Gielgud directing a Broadway show. Suddenly in the middle of a scene, a loud vacuum cleaner was heard in the balcony. Sir John stopped the rehearsal, peered up to the balcony and in the kindest tone said "Oh cleaning lady, dear."

That story about the executive who American Express claims spent over two hundred thousand dollars in a strip club in one night – he says it was much less – raises an interesting question, I haven't seen discussed.

How on earth do you spend over two hundred thousand dollars in a night in a strip club? If you imagine the guy was drunk and kept stuffing huge amounts of money *down* somewhere, *that* can't be it, because these were credit card charges. Did he yell out "I'm buying a stripper to sit on every guys lap in the house?" No one says he did that! Did he buy the stripper's *cars*? *What?!*

That story about "Shamu the killer whale" dragging the guy who's been sitting on him for some time, under water and injuring him wasn't all that surprising. You sit on top of a killer whale long enough I can see where that could easily happen. I always wondered what kind of a guy *wants* to sit on top of a killer whale for a living.

I also wonder about guys or girls who work alongside different dangerous wild animals, or climb the highest mountains, or ski or motorcycle without a helmet or even *with* one. That's not me.

As I've said I'm a guy who wears long johns *indoors,* and when I think that I used to ride the big dipper at the amusement park I must have been nuts – or just young. Between 9/11, anthrax, talk of nuclear attacks, dirty bombs, the world seems plenty dangerous enough without sitting on top of a killer whale.

The television producer Norman Lear bought the Declaration of Independence for around eight million dollars. The next day I read in the paper, that it wasn't actually the Declaration of Independence Norman had bought, but one of

[271]

the few copies that were made at the signing.
Close enough. If the government's selling an
original copy of the Declaration, it's not to hard
to imagine that in really tough times, they will
sell the Declaration itself to Norman.

I've known Norman Lear for a long time. I've
tried to sell him a couple of scripts over the
years, but he wasn't buying. It never occurred to
me he was saving his money to buy the
Declaration. It's amazing what you can buy
these days. Michael Jackson bought some of
The Elephant Man's bones.

There was an English philosopher named Jeremy
Bentham, who endowed the University of
London with a lot of money and was on their
board. In his will he asked that after he passed
away, he be stuffed and brought in a glass case
to still attend the board meetings. He *was* too.
I've been to some board meetings, where
sometimes I wish *I* was stuffed.

I doubt there's anything in Jeremy Bentham's
will that would prohibit Norman Lear from
buying him. It just gives us all something else to
think about. Clearly The Elephant Man didn't
think of it. There should be a law that says

nobody can sell us, after we pass away. What if Norman next buys the Bill of Rights? We'd now have to wait for an invite to Norman's house to see the Bill, rather than just pop over to the Smithsonian or wherever the heck it was.

I used to be invited to Norman's house on a regular basis, but I haven't talked to him in years. Personally for me it would be awkward to call him and say, "Norman, I'm in the neighborhood, I wonder if I could drop by to see the Declaration of Independence."

Years ago I saw Tarik Aziz, a former high ranking official in Saddam Hussein's government testifying at the trial in his pajamas. It brought back to mind that when Saddam was captured he was hiding in a hole in the ground with our soldiers pointing their guns at him. Among his first words from the hole were "I'm willing to negotiate."

I knew the late Charles Bronson. I worked with him I think more than once in Westerns for television. One day a group of us were having lunch in the commissary at Universal pictures. Bronson's order came first, and he dug right in.

He was about half way finished, and the lunches for the rest of us still hadn't come. I looked at him and said "Why don't you start?" Everyone laughed, but Bronson just fixed me with a stare and said "Y'know if I ever have a problem with someone, I don't hit them. I just bite their jugular vein."

Another time in the makeup room very early in the morning people were chatting about this and that. Bronson was silent, until he said in a loud voice, "*Chit* chat, *chit* chat." All the chit chat stopped. I wrote about all of this in one of my books. Years later I ran into him at some event. He told me that some friends of his had felt he should sue me for telling those stories, but he felt it was all in fun. I assured him he was right. After my lunch encounter with Charles Bronson, I always assured him he was right – about everything!

When L. Dennis Kozlowski, the former Chairman of Tyco International was under indictment for stealing six hundred million dollars from Tyco. His lawyer recently made a request to seal videotapes of a party he gave in Sardinia for his wife's fortieth birthday, so potential jurors don't see them before Mr. Kozlowski's criminal trial begins.

At the party there was an ice sculpture of Michaelangelo's David with vodka streaming from its penis into crystal glasses. It's fascinating to see what some people think is a nice touch.

I've met a few billionaires in my time. My first was when I went to a party at a friend's house, and he whispered in my ear that a guy over in the corner was a billionaire. He had invented some kind of chip or something. I'm not sure why my friend pointed him out to me. It's not as though he was going to hand me some money, or anything. I actually later became friends with the guy. I've known him for years now, and he has *yet* to give me a dime.

I know Barry Diller. He's a billionaire. I always see his name and smiling face in the paper. There's usually a story about how he bought some company for three hundred million and later sold it for seven hundred million, but I have no idea what these companies do, or how Barry made four hundred million on the sale. Barry's never given me a dime either.

I know Ron Perlman. He owns Revlon, and I'm pretty sure he's a billionaire. He was on the phone at some event I was at recently. I asked him if he'd cut me in on a little piece of whatever he was talking about. He smiled and shook my hand so hard it still hurts.

I write for the New York Daily News website. The News is owned by Mort Zuckerman, whom I'm told is a billionaire. When we have lunch, Mort *always* gets the check. We're friends. I'm sure it has *something* to do with my never having asked Mort to throw a million or two my way.

The publishing house of Simon and Schuster once sued one of its authors, because they claim he's not as big a *criminal* as he claimed he was. The author is a man named Michael Pellegrino, a resident of Las Vegas who claimed to be the illegitimate grandson of the late Mafia boss Carlo Gambino.

According to an article in the New York Times the book was marketed as the work of the "highest ranking mob member ever to record the inner workings of the Mafia." In an interview on Good Morning America the author said that "Writing the book helps me cleanse my soul."

He was introduced as "A member of the most powerful crime family in New York." Current investigation of Mr. Pellegrino's criminal past reveals that he spent nineteen months in prison for misappropriation of a twenty four hundred dollar rental deposit. Mr. Pellegrino's attorney claims that his client has been charged in two separate cases of theft, where he has pled guilty. This has got to be a first – someone trying to *pad* their criminal background.

I was at the Post Office the other day, and the clerk who always has a kind of very serious expression asked me the usual questions, when I was mailing something. "Is there anything fragile, liquid, perishable or potentially hazardous in there? Do you want express mail, priority, parcel post? Do you want insurance in case of loss or damage? Would you like delivery confirmation and proof of mailing? Would you like other stamps, packaging products, prints, or retail items?" He then took a pause and said "Would you like some advice?"

F.M. Esfandiary was a renowned futurist who earlier had changed his name to F.M.-230. He would have turned one hundred in 2030. Many of his predictions came true. In 1977 he spoke of correcting genetic flaws and of fertilization and gestation outside the body.

In 1980 he wrote of coming teleconferencing, telemedicine and teleshopping. He felt we wouldn't need more nursing homes in the future, because health treatment would improve. Part of his futuristic vision is that one day we will be entirely made of synthetic parts.

He felt questions about his own age were impossible to answer, since he had a two year old hip replacement. He felt that traditional families would be replaced by a Club Med morality. A lot of dating. He never married, so that might have been wishful thinking.

He thought death was tyrannical and wanted to do away with it. Boy there's a campaign promise. If I'm elected… His body is currently frozen and under the care of a life extension foundation in Arizona.

The foundation noted in a news release that no frozen mammal has ever been successfully thawed. No money back guarantee there. F.M.-2030 who was known for his sunny optimism acknowledged that he would have no money if he woke, but said he wouldn't care, because he would be so glad he was back. He probably *knows* he would make a fortune on the lecture circuit.

According to a story in the New York Daily News, the former Vice Chairman of Walmart was sentenced to twenty seven months home detention for falsifying expense reports.

Walmart accused the Vice Chairman of wrongly claiming reimbursement for hundreds of thousands of dollars worth of items including hunting gear, dog food, underwear, beer jerky and a stuffed wild boar.

Reimbursement for a stuffed wild boar?! What was he thinking? The Vice Chairman will also get five years probation and pay four hundred eleven thousand two hundred and eighteen dollars in restitution to Walmart and the government. When the Vice Chairman joined the company in 1978, he was in charge of theft prevention.

I saw, I guess it was an infomercial for Tony Robbins who's a big handsome guy, who's also some kind of a guru. There's footage of what looks like thousands of people in stadiums standing waving their arms in the air and *screaming*!

Tony's on the stage throwing *his* arms into the air and yelling *something* like "You can reach your full potential!" Then it says Tony has met and advised all kinds of world leaders – There's video of Nelson Mandela in there – President Clinton – "Met and advised?" I think more met.

I've met President Clinton, but that's really about it in the world leader department. I've *never* advised him. Anyway they're presenting Tony Robbins as a good looking guru, who has advised world leaders and brings thousands of people to their feet waving their arms and screaming "We can reach our full potential." Look I'm not saying the guy's not a good guru, but there *is* such a thing as overkill. He really crossed the line when he got people to walk barefoot across hot coals to "Unleash the power within." Twenty one people suffered burns.

I was flipping around on my t.v. with the sound off the other night, when I saw New York's Mayor Bloomberg at a podium. I then watched, as he introduced Senator Fred Thompson of Tennessee who took the podium and was talking about terrorism. Then the camera showed the audience, and it was clear I wasn't watching a *press* conference, but a t.v. show in which the Mayor and the Senator were actors.

Actually as I've said, the Senator *was* an actor *before* he became a senator, and now he's an actor again – but then he ran for the nomination for the Republican party as president and didn't get it. I don't know if he's gone back to acting or is going to run for senator, or maybe he'll play a *role*, where he's a senator. At least, he stays busy.

There was a story in the news about how a sudden shift in the wind blew some people, who were riding in a balloon into a radio tower. *"A sudden shift in the wind?!"* Do you know how often you could have a sudden shift in the wind?

Don't you think it might be a good idea for you to be somewhere other than in a *balloon*, when that happens? The people in the balloon were entangled in the tower, and they were helped down. Amazingly they escaped unharmed. If you were them, would you try it again? Would *you* want to try it? Who are these people who travel around in a balloon? Balloon salesmen? Travel in a balloon subject to a sudden shift in the wind? Not me!

I once saw two stories running at the bottom of the page of a newspaper the other day, and I was trying to figure out which one was…I can't find the words. One was about the father of a pee wee football player – these are six and seven year olds – the father of one of the children pulled a *gun* on the coach, because he was angry about the amount of playing time the little boy was getting – he pulls a gun. Uh huh.

The other story was about twenty six year old porn star Mary Carey, who said she was dropping out of the race for the California governorship to be with her mom, who's in the hospital since leaping off a four story building last month.

The young porn star said "As much as I want to help the state of California to be a better place, I think it's more important to be with my mom" – unless not to be cruel, the mom leapt off the four stories, for among other reasons, *because* her daughter is a twenty six year old porn star, who wants to be the Governor of California.

Some guy, who wrote a book about the late famed basketball coach, John Wooden once said in a radio interview, "If everybody could spend a couple of hours with Coach Wooden, our country would be problem free."

Not just better off – problem *free*! I guess the host is just more polite than I am, because I would have said "Problem *free*?" I loved Coach Wooden, and I would have loved to spend a couple of hours with him, and I'm sure I would benefit from those two hours, but I honestly don't think I'd suddenly become problem free. You haven't heard my *problems*!

This one, over the years has stayed with me. In the all things are relative department, New Jersey Net basketball player Kenyon Martin wanted to be traded. Why? According to his agent, Kenyon loves New Jersey, his teammates, and coaches. He does a lot of charitable work in New Jersey and wants to be part of it, *but* he also wants to be *secure* for the rest of his career.

What's the problem? Reportedly the Nets offered him a six year contract extension worth around sixty five million dollars. The *problem* is they could have offered him eighty seven million. If sixty five million doesn't make you feel secure, it begs the question – what is it you want to *buy*?

According to Mark Humphrey's, a genealogy enthusiast and professor of computer science at Dublin City University in Ireland, we're *all* descended from royalty in a fairly distant way – of course. According to Professor Humphrey one of King Edward III descendants is Humphrey Bogart.

Here's my problem with all of this. I've never really bought into the whole royalty thing. Don't get me wrong. When I've met royalty – I'm *very nice*, but I'm very nice, even if you're *not* royalty.

A recent article I read in the New York Daily News says Brook Shields is a descendant of the Medicis, Popes, Charlemagne and William the Conqueror. So if it makes people happy to feel they're descended from royalty, I'm happy for you. But if you told me, you were a descendant of say William the Conqueror, I'd kind of be on my guard a little bit.

I am really fascinated by the radio psychologist, Dr. Laura Schlesinger. Granted she is bright and can have useful insights and can on occasion perform a valuable service. The problem I have is with her all knowingness. There rarely seems to be any question that what she's saying could possibly be anything less than 100% right.

Even though she talks to people only for a few minutes, she is more than willing to tell them what to do about something, that could impact on the rest of their life. Leave your husband, leave your wife questions? No problem, here's what you should do. Sometimes she'll tell you within a minute.

It hardly ever seems to occur to her that the picture she's getting may not be the full truth. Most people in describing a problem can't get the full truth out in five minutes, if we're *ever* capable of seeing it. She's recently infuriated many people with what she's had to say about homosexuality.

Of course, Dr. Laura is entitled to her views, but one of them seems to be if only gay people would exercise discipline they could be heterosexual, and if they don't, well, as I understand her, they shouldn't feel too good about themselves.

And while I personally would not want to be involved with abortion, I really thought it was poor judgment on the doctor's part to make a young woman caller, who'd had an abortion feel so bad about herself; probably for life.

The despair she brought to this twenty year old, who was already badly upset was unforgivable. Also she's made a lot of working mothers furious lately, suggesting they couldn't possibly work regularly and be Dr. Laura's concept of the right kind of mother. Oh, she tells us it can be done if mother and father take off from their jobs and share the responsibility for their children. That comes under the heading of "Nice work if you can get it."

Dr. Laura, of course, controls where she works, so she can properly look after her children. For me personally looking back as a kid, I don't think I'd much want a role model who seems to know everything about everything, and if I did have one, I sure wouldn't want them around *all the time.*

There doesn't seem to be anything Dr. Laura doesn't know. I heard her tell a caller the other day that "Most people when they do sit ups, really work their hip muscles instead of their stomach muscles." Perish the thought. Somebody should call and ask "What do you do if you live with someone who presents themselves as knowing *everything* about *everything*?" That's an answer I'd like to hear.

The other day I was offered a considerable amount of money just to show up and mingle at a party in Philadelphia. Not to speak. Just to mingle. I couldn't do it. I imagined myself mingling, and I'm sure more than one person there would have asked what brought you here? "Are you a friend of the host?" "No, I've never met him, I'm here because they paid me to come and mingle." I stayed home.

[287]

It all brought to mind another time when I was not only not paid but told if showed up, I'd be thrown out of the building. When I was beginning in show business, through a distant family connection, I was able to get a meeting with a major casting director in New York. The woman seemed very pleased to meet me, said I seemed like just the kind of young person she liked to reach out to, a serious dedicated fellow.

I assured her I was, and she said she'd be in touch in a few weeks and would be able to place me in a very small guest role on a popular weekly police drama she cast. I walked out of her office at least one inch off the ground. This was in a period that no one had any interest in placing me in anything other than on a line to see if there was a cab available for me to drive, which is what I was doing at the time.

On the way to the elevator I ran into a young woman I knew from an acting class we had taken. She turned out to now be working as the casting director's assistant. She seemed surprised to see me, and when I told her of the meeting, she said "I remember you as someone who took a lot of pauses, when you did scenes in class."

She *didn't* mean it as a compliment. I instantly became uneasy and assured her that I could go as fast as anyone wanted me to, and all those past long pauses would certainly present no.....She didn't seem to be listening, and as she walked away, I swallowed hard, and said it was really nice to see her.

After about a month of not hearing from the casting director, I called my former class mate, and asked if I could take her to lunch. She said she didn't eat lunch in such a way I chose not to ask about dinner. I let another few weeks of silence from the casting director go by, before I wrote what I thought was a very friendly letter reminding her of our meeting and told of meeting her assistant and the pauses issue.

I assured her there'd be no problem with pauses, and hoped I would still hear from her. What I heard instead from an agent was that the casting director told him, if I as much as show up in the lobby of the building, where she had her office she'd have me thrown out! I showed the letter I had written to a couple of friends to see if I had

[289]

missed something, but no it was a pleasant letter of a young man looking for a job.

I can only assume that what angered her was it was also a gentle reminder of a broken promise. Years later when I was working enough that people had heard of me, I ran into her a couple of times, and she couldn't have been nicer. Neither of us mentioned the past. In all this time I've never run into her assistant, my former classmate. I know she went on to be a producer.

If I did run into her, I probably wouldn't recognize her, and if she introduced herself, I'd probably smile and be pleasant to her as well. Oh, I'm not saying I wouldn't work in a long pause.

Recently a man set a new world's record for kissing a cobra. He kissed a cobra's head fifty one times. I saw video on it. He was smiling too. The previous record was eleven kisses. I'm not sure why he stopped. Maybe he felt the cobra was getting on to his move. You might kiss a cobra fifty one times, but if he kisses you *once* – forget about it! I don't know what the guy does for a living or even if he makes one,

but he's not your boy next door. Maybe
someday he'll go into politics.

Once when I was watching CNN, and I saw
Anderson Cooper swimming among sharks.
Oddly enough, *I* swam among sharks when I was
way out in the Pacific Ocean while attending the
University of Miami in Florida.

The difference between Anderson and me is I
didn't *know* I was doing it. I only realized it
later. Swim among sharks? That's just not me.
Oh, don't get me wrong, I'll go down *stairs* in
the evening, but let's not push it all the way to
swim among sharks.

Can the world get any stranger? I'm sure it can.
First we have the guy who's alleged to have
faked his son being up in a balloon when he
wasn't -- looking for maybe a t.v. appearance,
that could lead to a series.

The wildest for me is the former congressman
Tom DeLay who was an exterminator, before he
was elected to Congress, then he became known
as the Hammer. *Then* he's kicked out of
Congress, because of illegalities, *then* while out

on bail he's on *Dancing With the Stars*, where he not only loses, but fractures both of his feet.

A friend of mine told me he recently received a letter from a man in Nigeria, who was annoyed with him because he hadn't sent the man ninety dollars which would in return get my friend nine hundred and ninety thousand dollars. Right. Oh boy!

Over the years we've had several various nice gentlemen out to the house to fix that loud noise our refrigerator makes. They fix it too, for about a day, and then another nice man appears and wonders what on earth his predecessor was thinking and then another, and then another. The phrase "stuck in the same job for a long time" always had a negative ring to it, but those are the people I want. They probably know how to do it.

A man in Saudi Arabia, who I assume had been complaining about stomach pain had a toothbrush removed from his stomach, that he had swallowed *twenty two years ago*. In the truly off chance that actually happened, it does cry out for more questions. Did he know he swallowed a toothbrush twenty two years ago?

By the way, he wasn't a child then. Why suffer with it for twenty two years? How do you swallow a tooth brush? Was it deliberate, an accident? Oh … gee …naah…until I hear more, I don't believe it.

Some of you probably have heard about that unidentified flying object – that slammed into a house in New Jersey. The golf ball size hunk punched right through the roof, then hit the floor of a second story bathroom and ended up in a wall. The town's police department claimed the object belonged to the township, not the family, as it was part of an ongoing investigation.

I don't know…if a rock like thing crashes through your roof, and lands in your bathroom wall, with all due respect to the police's ongoing investigation, I'd say it's yours. Crashes through your roof and lands in your bathroom and it's *not* yours?! Naah…it's yours. There's a happy ending to this story. Turns out it was a *meteor*, and the police department now concedes it belongs to the family. I just hope they can sell it to cover the costs of fixing the roof, and their wall, and have a few bucks left over for tranquilizers.

I read a story in the paper recently about how this family's pet snake, three feet long somehow got out of their apartment, traveled up four flights of stairs got into another apartment and tightly wrapped itself around the arm of a sleeping three year old boy. The snake's owner argued that the snake is only *two* feet long and "only as wide as my pinky."

He then seemed to ridicule the housekeeper, who saw this, again quoting the owner "They have this housekeeper, who sees the snake and goes ballistic – "Oh my God!" and starts screaming." According to this man, if your snake gets out of your apartment and goes into another apartment and wraps itself around a sleeping child, it's not *that* big a deal. There are millions of people all over the world, who claim to be never wrong about *anything*!

A recent story in the New York Post caught my attention. A woman climbing a 380 foot cliff in a park in New Haven, Connecticut couldn't get *down* once she got up. She called for help on her *cell* phone I assume, because there are very few phone booths on cliff tops.

The fire department rescued her, and the police billed her for $6,000 for violating a city ordinance barring the climb and four counts of reckless endangerment for jeopardizing the fire fighters. Two questions. First; was there a sign forbidding her to climb the 380 foot cliff? Second; who *is* this woman anyway?

Marius Varga, a twenty three year old Romanian man stopped some police and told them he had killed a friend and wanted to give himself up. After the police questioned him, it turned out he had spent all his money drinking and basically made up the story, because he needed a ride home.

A Brooklyn judge who normally handles domestic violence cases and orders defendants to take anger management classes stormed off the bench, went nose to nose with a lawyer, grabbed him by both arms and screamed "This is my courtroom. You will do as I say!" The case was about a parking ticket. And *he's* telling people to go to anger management classes?

Sometimes the simplest things are beyond my understanding. In my area, there's a street sign, and under the street sign there's kind of like a subtitle that says Possum Lane. Does that mean there are two streets there? Does it mean the main street has so many possum, an agent for the possum got the Possum Lane sub title?

Even more confusing there's a road called Skunk Lane. If you lived on Skunk Lane, don't you think you could get your neighbors to sign a petition asking for a name change? Am I the only one out there, who would prefer the name of my lane not be Skunk? Don't get me wrong. I don't live on Skunk Lane. I'm saying, *if* I lived on Skunk Lane.

Recently I went into my local market. There was a sign on the door saying it was the birthday of someone working back in the meat department and asked customers to wish him a happy birthday. I went back to do it. I asked which one of you guys has a birthday today? One man raised his hand, so I wished him a happy birthday.

I asked if he liked going through the day having strangers wish him a happy birthday. He shrugged and gave me the impression he could take it or leave it. A man standing nearby said "You know who you sound like?"

I said, "Yeah everyone says that to me. Actually I am him." He didn't believe me, so I showed him identification. He said "I listen to you on the radio all the time. What would *you* be doing here?" At first I thought he wondered why someone on the radio would need to *eat*, but of course, he meant he didn't know I lived in the area.

I appeared at a recent event held by Help U.S.A. It was to raise money for housing for homeless female veterans from Iraq and Afghanistan. "Homeless female veterans from Iraq and Afghanistan." Oh brother.

I showed some comedy clips from my cable show from fifteen years ago. A man in the audience shouted out "You look older now." There's a breaking news story. "Man looks *older* fifteen years later."

It reminds me of something that happened a few years ago. A makeup woman was taking my makeup off after a television appearance. She whispered into my ear "Who did your work? I don't see any scars." I said "I haven't had any work done." She then asked "Was it someone in Los Angeles?" I again said "I haven't had any work done." She then whispered to me "I won't tell anyone." Again I said "I haven't had any work done." She *never* believed me. Some things just come under the heading of "What are you gonna do?"

AWARDS AND HONORS

"Don't get me wrong."

I got an award recently. I'm very proud of it.

I'm not going to say what it's for. I think it's bad enough I'm even saying I *got* an award. When I first heard I was going to get this award, I actually tried to talk the organization out of *giving* me the award. I said there are people way more deserving of this award than I am but they *insisted* – so I accepted the award.

Don't get me wrong. I've gotten awards in the past, but this for me is the *best* award I've ever gotten. It's in the form of a bronze metal. I've always kept my awards upstairs, but this one I slipped downstairs. My wife was kind enough to come up with a nice stand for my prized bronze disc award. A friend came over recently and spotted it. I told him why I got it, and how proud I was to have it. He looked at it and said "**Bronze?** It's like you came in *third.*"

I'm always interested when I see schools, stadiums, office buildings, highways named after different people. I never wanted anything like that, because I assume you have to be deceased to get it – for the most part anyway. I'm sure there are some exceptions if you're just really *old*, but I bet that's very hard to get.

Anyway, in my area we have the Jackie Robinson Parkway. Lately I'm hearing the parkway referred to as the *Jackie*. *That* I really don't want. I could maybe get a highway in my area, if I'm ever gone, but I don't want The Charles Grodin Highway. Soon they'd say there's a big crash on the Chuck. Naah. I don't want it.

I was being interviewed about something the other day and the youngish interviewer referred to me as a legend. The word legend has been really loosely used lately regarding all *kinds* of people, who have been around a long time, so a few months ago I looked it up in the dictionary.

Here's the definition of a legend "One popularly accepted as historical, but *not* verifiable." I feel the not verifiable part applies to me. I mean who among us is going to say they're historical, which is defined as "important or famous in *history*." Don't look at me, boss.

The late Peter Falk once wrote in a book about going into a deli, and a waiter said to him

"There's a lot of legends in here today." He meant older comics. We love our entertainers, but I think we may be throwing around legend a little too loosely. Let's stay with the not verifiable part.

FAMILY

"Not everything from the kids is wisdom."

I've been fortunate enough to appear in movies. Over the years, I've gotten more than my share of compliments but being given an opportunity to offer my opinions on the *radio* these past twelve years has been the most rewarding media experience I've ever had. People came up to me to let me know they agree with my opinion. With all due respect to being in the movies, if people say to you "I agree with your opinion" *that's something – especially* if you're married with kids.

When I was a kid my favorite uncle was my Uncle Bob. When we would visit my family in Chicago, Uncle Bob always took us kids everywhere and always had a good spirit about everything – including life advice. Uncle Bob became my uncle role model, so when I had nieces and nephews visit this summer, I've tried to be like my Uncle Bob.

The other evening I was sitting in a room with my thirteen year old nephew and eleven year old niece. I told them that in order to get where you want to get in life you have to work hard, study hard and give it your best, because life can be difficult, and giving your best – in their case in school was very important.

They were just kind of staring at me not saying a word. I really couldn't tell what they were thinking. Then their dad came in, and I told him what I'd been telling the kids about working hard in school etc. He said very nicely they were both straight A students and had even already won some awards. I congratulated them and took a walk.

Years ago, I came downstairs in the evening ready to have some fun with my fourteen year old son, who was very involved with something on his computer. If I've got this right, he was ordering a CD from a rap group, who doesn't have a deal with a music company, but sells their stuff on the internet, where my kid buys C.D.'s, posters, sweatshirts.

The guys doing this, who are just starting *give* you a lot of free stuff you don't even have to ask for. Anyway, I sat there watching all this, waiting for an opening to ask him how he's doing or get to tell him how I'm doing, but he looked at me, sensed what I was up to and quickly said, "Why don't you wait in the den? I'll be in in about ten minutes."

I nodded, and walked into the kitchen, pulled up a chair, looked at my wife, who looked back at me, also sensing what I was up to and said, "Oh, were you going to…Uh, I was just heading upstairs." I politely nodded at her, and she went upstairs.

Because of them, I've just finished my fifth book, get to say what I think on radio as well as in a new play I've written, which is my sixth. If the people at home would have just sat down and listened to me whenever I wanted, I probably wouldn't have written anything.

I always perk up when I hear someone say – my mother always told me or my father always said – as though if a parent says it – it's gospel. The other day I heard someone on the radio say "My father always told me "Look out for number one."

He went on to say his father meant, if you don't look out for yourself – no one else is going to, which may or may not be true. Another way of looking at it is if you look out for others – maybe more people will look out for – or at least *care* about you. I once had a guy for reasons only known to him tell me, if I ever wanted to hijack a trailer truck, I should hijack one carrying razor blades. He said quite earnestly "Do you realize how many razor blades you can get on a trailer truck?" I wonder if he was a dad.

A friend of mine and his wife were trying to get their three and a half year old daughter into a preschool, but there were no openings, so she had to go to another preschool, which she didn't like. My friend started to hang out with the people at the church next door to the preschool, where his three and a half year old wanted to go.

Pretty soon she's in, but she felt shut out for so long, that when she first arrived, she announced to the representative of the school "My brother just peed on your rug. He's a terrorist."

Her brother was one. The moral of this story is the more you shut people out the more it can come back to bite you even from three and a half year olds. Whenever possible *include* rather than exclude. Excluding can often come back at you in more serious ways than a one year old boy peeing on your rug.

[307]

I was standing in front of this huge deli counter
at the market the other day, when I heard a kid,
who looked around ten say to his mother
"Wouldn't it be neat if they took all this food..."
At that point his mother interrupted him to ask
the guy behind the counter a question.

I thought to myself you gotta let kids talk,
express themselves – we can all learn from the
kids. That's where real wisdom can come from.
The boy started up again "Wouldn't it be neat if
they took all of this food and dumped it on
someone's head?" Well, of course, not
everything from the kids is wisdom.

When I was a kid, my three most prized
possessions were first a red pedal machine, I
remember tooling around in when I was four.
Next was my flexible flyer sled, and then came
my blue and white bike, a Schwinn two wheel –
a big one. I have *none* of those prized
possessions now. I promise you, *I* didn't give
them away.

I'm not naming names here because of the love
in my heart, but *someone* either *gave away* or
left behind my peddle machine, my sled, and my
bike. Keep an eye on your prized possessions,

and let anyone and everyone know they are not to be given away – at least not without your prior consultation.

My daughter, who's a stand-up comic, called me recently to see, if we should get together for Father's Day, or should she play a club? She called, because she knew I *don't* celebrate Father's Day or other holidays.

To me *every* day should be Mother's Day, Father's Day or whatever *you* think *deserves* a day. In other words whatever you do on those special days should *always* be done every day. Of course, that doesn't include staying home from work.

I think we should all give thanks that we don't have to have approval ratings around our own house. I mean a lot of us do at work but thankfully not at home. Imagine what your *approval rating* would be just before your spouse decides they've had enough – or the way your kids sometimes look at you. What if everyone in a family had to post their approval rating of everyone else in a family at the end of each day? What a nightmare that would be.

RELATIONSHIPS

"Nothing's easy."

Happily, it's been my experience that I get along with people very well.

There are only two people I can think of in my whole life that I would dearly wish never to see or speak to again, and there's a long list of people who feel as I do toward these infamous two. So I was taken aback the other day, to get a very angry message from a woman who claimed I lied – she said I misrepresented myself and she was going to call the police! Turned out it was a wrong number. But it was a reminder of what could happen to you if you *don't* treat people well.

My brother told me a story recently about how he and his wife were out for dinner with another couple. He said the wife of the other couple never stopped talking. At one point my brother began to tell a story to her husband.

The woman interrupted him saying "You've told that story before." My brother didn't take that kindly saying "I wasn't talking to you. *You've* been talking all night." Later my brother heard that the woman felt he didn't like her. She said

"How can he not like me? *Everybody* likes me."
Two points here: If *everybody* likes you, it
means you never take a *stand* on anything. Also
never tell anyone they've told a story before.
We *all* eventually will do it. Cut slack.

The moment the law allowed same sex couples
to marry it was inevitable that there would be a
same sex divorce. Approximately half of
opposite sex marriages end in divorce – so it's
not exactly *breaking* news there would be a
same sex divorce. Put two people together --
same sex – opposite sex – married or not – and
you're going to at *least* have *some* trouble – and
that goes for *animals* too.

Being an advocate for those I feel are unjustly in
prison, I sometimes am in court. Recently I was
there in a child support case for a woman for
whom I gained clemency.

While waiting for her case to be called, I heard
the judge say to a man in another case "I'm not
criticizing you, I'm puzzled by you." I thought
what a great line to use to try to avoid arguments
in my life. "I'm not criticizing you, I'm puzzled
by you." Try it. It *might* lead to calmer
discourse.

[313]

According to my local paper – in town there are
groups representing *whatever* going at each
other like tigers, swearing, even *pushing*. I told
this to a friend of mine who said he knows two
neighbors who are suing each other, because one
feels the other's child swing set swings over
their property line – and on and on and *on*.

It reminds me of something a very bright young
man said to his wife. They once entered a large
gathering and she counted *26* people she felt she
had to confront . He said to her "Turn it over."
You could say "move on," "let it go." You can't
always be in turmoil over *what*? Turn it over.
You'll live longer.

I have a longtime friend whose grandson calls
me Uncle Charley. The other day I asked the
little boy how old he was. He said "Five and a
half." I asked "When will you be six?" He said
in true amazement "You mean you don't know,
Uncle Charley?" When we're very young, it's
not unique to believe the world revolves around
us. The problem is there are too many people
who continue to believe that at any age.

A young woman wrote to an advice columnist with a problem that *never* occurred to me. She says she's attractive, in good health and in excellent shape, *but* she has reason to believe she's *stronger* than her fiancée! In any case, she can beat him at wrestling! Talk about things that generally don't come up in a relationship. Can I *beat* you up?

I've never thought of that. Get along with – care about – love – *that* I've thought about. Beat up? Why would any man or woman want to go *there*? Go figure.

We all like to have fun. Some of us work at it a little harder than others. Years ago before I was married I would make some fun plan for the evening's activity, often filling every night for about ten days ahead of time. Usually it was just arranging to be with groups of friends and it was fun. These days I go out a lot less, but I still always try to have a fun plan for the evening, and I try to spruce up the day time activity as well. I do this by kidding around more than say your average person.

About ten years ago I started asking the person who takes your money at a toll booth if they sold ice cream there. It always got a blank stare followed by a laugh. I've been going into a Sam Goody music store lately.

As you walk in, there's a young woman there who says "Welcome to Sam Goody's." The next time I go in, after she says "Welcome to Sam Goody's," I plan to say "Thank you. I'd like a table in the back by a window." It may not get a laugh, but I'm going to try it. I know this may sound silly to some, but I don't think so.

The last time I was in the local post office it was empty with just three clerks standing there. I said accusatorily "O.K, which one of you is responsible for that last rate hike on stamps?" They all laughed. It may not have made their day, but it sure didn't hurt.

A judge and his wife, who's an attorney, were on television. The reason they were on is the wife was running against her husband for his position as judge! The judge said he thought he'd done a very good job on the bench for the last twenty-one years. His wife didn't say he hadn't. His position was the only one up for reelection and she said running against her husband for his job as judge was the only way *she* could be a judge.

In other words "Why is he the only one who gets to judge?" She sat there looking very happy about the whole thing and said in so many words that she wanted to reach her full potential etc., etc., etc. Her husband the judge, sat there really trying to look o.k., and again said he thought he'd done a very good job.

I don't know. I realize the job market is tough, but to go after your spouse's job?! I can't believe their relationship will be the same *after* the election. If *he* wins, I'll bet she's not smiling as much. If *she* wins, he'll be unemployed. And you think you have problems in *your* marriage?

The other night I started to think about forming a posse – y'know, like those rock singers have – a three guy entourage if you will, and I've got the perfect three guys. They all happen to be big strong guys – former football players – linemen – one played in college.

They're all incredibly good natured – love to have a good time – but sensible. They all went to school longer than I did. One even graduated Yale. The posse with these three guys would be tremendous. Lots of laughs and good times.

[317]

Here's the problem. They live in California. Two of them anyway, and the guy who lives closer to me…well one guy's not a posse. Unless I wanted to hire them and have them all live near me, I don't see how it can work. Besides you really want a posse if you're going out.

The problem is I almost *never* go out, and I don't need one at home. The posse concept at this point in my life doesn't really work, but for you guys or girls who *do* go out, I think it's a good idea. Most of you have probably thought about it already, but for those of you who haven't thought about it – think about it.

Here's something that really makes me nervous. I'm talking to someone, and suddenly without even realizing what's hitting me, they're telling me the story of some movie they saw. "And then they go up this hill, and at the top of the mountain they look down and see this little village – so they go down the other side of the mountain -- and they see this man in front of a house," and on and on and *on*! Why do people do that?

I'm sure it's *happened* to most of you – some of *you* may even *do* it. Don't *do* it – unless you're in a *film* class, and someone *asks* you to do it. Let me be *perfectly* clear! Don't describe a movie, a book or play, *unless* someone asks you to. I'm not swearing to this, but *no one* will *ever* ask.

A guy wrote the following to an advice columnist. "My new girlfriend spent the night at my place for the first time this past weekend. When we got up, I prepared breakfast while she made the bed, so we could head to work at the same time.

Later that evening upon my return to my apartment, I found her eyeliner pencil on my dresser. Do you think that was a ploy, or did she just accidentally leave it? I don't want to overreact, but I don't like that behavior at all." Here's *my* advice to his girlfriend. "Do not walk, *run* away from this guy – run!"

A headline on a sports column in USA Today said "Coach Told to Stop Hypnotizing Team." Good. The coach of the St. John's boy's high school basketball team in Kansas had been hypnotizing his players, until the St. John school board voted to end the hypnosis session. We don't understand hypnosis well enough to do that. I mean he could be hypnotizing the young men to play strong defense.

This *could* somehow pop up later in relationships and marriages, which is a good way to end things. Relationships last because people make accommodations – *strong defense* is great in basketball, but in life can often cause divorce.

I keep thinking about that fella that went over Niagara Falls some time ago on an "impulse." People kill people on an impulse. People are constantly saying or doing something hurtful to someone else on an impulse.

The only place I can think of where acting on an impulse is most often called for is in sports. Athletes often don't have time to consider all the possibilities. Acting on impulse in life? I think you're better off walking around the block.

In the ten seconds I listened to the inaugural being broadcast on the radio, I heard a woman say something to the effect of "We need more than marital love. We need love of all kinds."

She somehow rhymed it, so it was considered a poem. Since more than half of marriages end in divorce, I started thinking of the extremely slight difference of letters in the words marital and martial.

They have exactly the same letters except the i comes before the t in marital and after the t in martial, which means "war like." Marriage *can* be war like. Those of us who prevail bring more love than war. Love of *any* kind. For example, no matter what you feel toward your partner, make the friendliest response you can. Do that and you can have a *marital* connection instead of *martial* one.

I saw an item from the Associated Press recently I had to read three times just to make sure I got it, and I'm *still* not sure. A woman accused of trying to poison her husband is moving back in with him, while she awaits trial.

If convicted she faces life in prison. Her husband said "Marriage is a terrible thing to throw away, if you don't have to." I don't know…I assume it was the *husband* who brought charges *against* the wife, that she was trying to poison him, *but* they're back together.

That husband is a heck of a lot more easygoing that *I* am. In those circumstances I can't see myself reading the paper and calling out "Honey, is dinner ready yet?"

The other day, just out of curiosity I took a look at some personal ads in the Times. I say just out of curiosity, because fortunately I'm a long time happily married man. They have a section called women seeking men, men seeking women, men seeking men, and women seeking women.

Times really have changed. One woman in her 60's, who is a general's widow is seeking, "Another tall General or equivalent." I guess that would mean a tall Admiral. He also must like animals and be non hirsute, which means non hairy. Okay.

A man who describes himself as a "Tall but interactive devil needs a muse to inspire him as he writes, makes art, etc." Another ad was "On behalf of my great uncle, and I mean great who is 91 and says the perfect woman should be Jewish or gentile." Uh huh.

Another entry is from a woman who describes herself as a beautiful loving sexy goddess, who wants a man who would help her with "some new career goals which include recording a song."

When people get to that point where maybe they start to think about having a life partner – I *think* most people think of some kind of physical attraction, or maybe just as many people think about degree of compatibility.

If you really get along, maybe have some laughs that could possibly *lead* to maybe a little physical attraction. But there may be a couple of necessities for a successful relationship, that don't get enough if *any* focus.

How loud or soft do you want the t.v.? How cold or warm do you want the temperature in your home? With all due respect to physical attraction and compatibility, these are important considerations in choosing a life partner, and I feel they're *wildly* overlooked. Of course, what makes it even more complicated is your desired volume and temperature change as time goes by. Nothing's easy.

A very close friend of mine called me recently and said he was facing a question, and he asked himself "What would Charley do?" He calls me Charley. I don't really see myself as a Charley. The only Charley I ever knew was always slapping everyone on the back and making inappropriate sexual comments.

Anyway, my close friend was facing a moral dilemma and he asked himself "What would Charley do?" I thought, wait a minute. What do I know about moral behavior that he doesn't? I mean, I kind of look to *him* for wisdom. Anyway, the moral question had to do with money, and the answer was do what's *fair* for everyone. He got that without even calling Charley. Easier said than to figure out *what's* fair even for Charley here.

It feels as though divorce is in the news more than usual lately. I saw a billboard recently saying "Life is short. Get a divorce." Then the other day I was in the shower, and the radio was on, and I heard a guy shout "I want a divorce."

I don't know what the context was – probably a promo for something. Is divorce suddenly getting more popular? It's my understanding that somewhere around half of all married people *already* are divorced or getting divorced. Of course, people who are *alone* most of the time don't seem to be jumping for joy either.

I was talking to a woman friend of mine about how much I admired the wife of another older friend. I said I admired how much she doted on him. "Yes dear, no dear, can I get you anything, dear?" My woman friend immediately challenged me with "Do you think women are the only ones who should dote?"

"Not at all," I said. "I think men should dote as well." I think couples should dote on each other. That's not to say we should be each other's servants or never express disagreement but given the strain we're all under, I think people who really care about each other *should* dote on each other. Let's call it mutual doting – within reason.

I was in a small social group the other day where three of the people didn't speak English. Since that's all I speak or understand, there was just a lot of smiling and nodding going on between us. Very pleasant. It reminded me of a movie

executive I knew years ago, who married a
beautiful woman from Czechoslovakia.

They were a very happy couple. The joke was
as soon as she learned English, they'd divorce,
and that's exactly what happened. When you
think of all the arguments we get into, because
we *understand* what the other person is saying, it
makes you wonder about the *value* of language.
Obviously we need it, but sometimes……

OTHER SPECIES

"Tell my parrot I'll call him back."

Early every morning a convention of crows

convene outside by bedroom window. I've tried
a lot of things to discourage them – fake owls
just made them scream louder. Finally I solved
the problem by waking up before they do.

I find people who hold themselves, as though
they're more important than others silly at best.
These so called elitists never learned that it's not
your station in life that matters – it's your
character. Elitism isn't just practiced by people,
there's also evidence it can be a function of
reindeer as well. Rudolph the red-nosed
reindeer was always made fun of by the other
reindeer, because he had a shiny red nose. They
laughed and called him names. They *never* let
Rudolph join in any reindeer games, but on one
foggy Christmas Eve, when Santa came and saw
Rudolph, he said "Rudolph with your nose so
bright, won't you guide my sleigh tonight?"
Then all the reindeer loved him. *Sure*, with
Santa on board. Sadly elitism is everywhere.

Specially trained dogs have been used to *excellent* results to sniff out hidden explosives. I feel we should train more and more and have them in *every* airport. Some people have complained they don't want a dog sniffing them all over. Of course, if you're not in possession of explosives, they move right on. This is what I call a no-brainer. Another complaint against using dogs is at some point they need to rest and need food. Wow! Dogs *are* demanding!

I saw a recent photograph in the paper of a baby elephant trying to get a drink from a dried up watering hole in Africa and then have a crocodile bite down on his trunk. The baby elephant screamed in horror and a group of adult elephants heard it and drove off the crocodile. That's what friends are for. You can't have too many friends, whether you're a person *or* an elephant.

Four horses competing in the Athens Olympics have tested positive for banned substances. Of course athletes have been dealing with this issue for years. Often they say they received treatment for legitimate medical reasons, not to improve performance. The horse's riders said "The horses received treatment for legitimate medical reasons, not to improve performance." The horses declined comment.

In a recent debate over whether dogs should be able to run around in the park or *anywhere* without a leash, some guy came up with the weirdest rationale for no leashes. He said dogs running around freely get tired from all the exercise, and are less likely to attack another dog or person. Yeah. Right. What about *before* they got too tired?

For years there have been so many instances of dogs off leashes attacking other dogs and people and children that I find it hard to believe it's a debatable subject. I still remember when I was a little kid looking out the window and seeing this dog – his name was Fuzzy, and he'd be walking alone down the street all the time, never with a person.

I don't know if Fuzzy ever attacked anyone, but the look on his face alone kept *this* little kid from approaching. In fact, I never saw anyone approach Fuzzy, who always seemed to be on some serious mission. Dogs running around off leashes? Cats maybe. Dogs? No way. And by the way I'm sure the cats agree with me.

I lived in New York City more than half of my life. Now I live in Fairfield County in Connecticut, a county *known* for its upscaleness. And yet no one in New York *ever screamed* at me for going to an open cash register, while this so called gentleman was waiting on another line. I told a couple of people ahead of me there was an open register, but no one moved. I was in and out with my one item, before *he* finished his tirade.

The other people were embarrassed to be on the same line as this...gentleman. No one in New York City ever accused me of being *idiotic*. The lady's' exact words were "Sir, that was *so* idiotic!" She was ripping me for something only *she* was aware of, that had evidently just happened in this infamously small parking area of this mall.

Obviously since I didn't drive a car around New York City, I couldn't have motorists scream at me for reasons known only to them or have a young man yell "Moron" at me, because I chose not to stop to have my car washed in response to his sign. I do spend some time in New York

City and to this day – nothing like that has ever happened. Worst of all I don't remember the Connecticut Chamber of Commerce mentioning there were bears on the loose. I never saw a bear on the street in all my decades in New York City.

It's estimated there are between 300 and 500 bears living in Connecticut right now. The Department of Environmental Protection has issued a warning to people to *take down bird feeders*. Take down bird feeders?! I bet we'll hear from the bird lobby on that one.

They advise *if you see a bear, exercise good judgment*. O.k. Good judgment. That's what I'm going to exercise. O.k. *Make your presence known by making a noise and waving your arms. Walk away slowly while facing the bear. Avoid direct eye contact*. O.k. I'm comfortable with that. No eye contact. *Black bears will sometimes bluff a charge and stop within a few feet of you. If this happens, stand your ground and shout at the bear*. And finally, *try to stay calm*. So wave your arms, shout at the bear, try to stay calm and hope the bear charging towards you is bluffing. Sometimes, I *do* miss New York.

I read an article in USA Today about how Britain's National Sea Life Center are piping Barry White music into the visitor's tunnel, that surrounds their shark tank in hopes it will put their celibate sharks in the mood for love, and they'll get some procreation going. Officials are hoping Barry's *"Can't Get Enough of Your Love, Babe"* and *"You're the First, the Last, My Everything"* will tempt the sharks into feeling more romantic. Not that I'm an authority on any of this, but I would suspect that Barry White might do the job more for the people in the visitor's tunnel than for the sharks.

Curator, Josie Sutherland said that after the first blast of Barry White, the sharks did seem to be a bit more excited and chased each other around the tank, but there were no signs of breeding yet. The curator said that if it didn't work on the sharks, that they would get an underwater speaker for the music. If it comes to that, I recommend they drop the Barry White and go for the theme from Jaws. If *that* doesn't get them going, nothing will. I mean it *was* a big hit movie starring a shark.

We're all familiar with how people like to stake out their territory, but the story about the pussy cat, who saw a big black bear enter its yard and chased the bear up a tree really is one for the books. And the bear *stayed* up in the tree while the little cat stood guard at the bottom, as though if that bear dared to climb down, it would be *very* sorry.

The bear eventually did climb down and ran off into the woods, probably when the cat looked away for a second to see if any other bears were around. It's a good idea to never underestimate the importance of a cat or anyone else's space.

I was watching a scientist interviewed the other day about this new concept of injecting human stem cells into sheep. The goal is to create transplantable organs from sheep into humans. When the question was raised about what might be the result of too many human stem cells into sheep, the scientist said "We'll worry about that when the sheep start talking back."

It's fascinating to me how people can be totally absorbed by such different things. On *60 Minutes* once there were all these people *more* than absorbed in their search for the Ivory billed woodpecker. I'd say more than absorbed, because millions have been spent on this search. Cornell University has eighteen thousand hours of recordings trying to *hear* if it's turned up anywhere.

One man said he's spent his whole life hoping, wondering, if the bird existed. He *wept* at stories of people describing having seen it, and said he would happily go to his grave, if we could save it. Look, I'm for saving endangered species as much as the next guy, but...*well*...whatever absorbs you.

When the Broadway musical *Tarzan* was about to open, I thought *this* I've gotta see.   Are they going to have Cheetah the monkey up there? If I remember correctly, Cheetah's a funny monkey. I can see where you could get that in a movie – but on stage? The swinging on the rope thing, I'm sure they can do, but didn't Tarzan regularly wrestle with and defeat wild animals? I decided not to go.

It's well established that America is the most violent of countries and, of course, like anyone I find that more than slightly unsettling. So I was actually relieved the other day to read a story in

[335]

the New York Times that in Turkey they have camel fighting! A Mr. Akmese was quoted as saying, "My camel is strong. He has a good body, good technique, and he knows how to use his front legs for tripping."

I learned from the article that winter is the only time of the year that camels will fight, because it's the mating season, and their instinct then is to knock each other down to win the right to "available females." I wasn't sure what the article meant by "available females" – as against *unavailable* females? "I'm sorry you're very nice, but I'm seeing another camel."

So in the winter these camels fight. The rest of the year, they just act like…camels. The article said, "A fight begins with two camels, the largest of which can weigh well over a ton being led toward each other. Sometimes one immediately bolts and runs away thereby forfeiting the match." That would be the smarter camel.

I mean, who wants to fight a camel, especially one who could weigh well over a ton and knows how to use his front legs for tripping? It's not logical, but the whole story somehow made me feel a tiny bit better about violence in America.

If you're a dog named *Bohem C'est La Vie,* also known as *Vivy*, and you just won a prize at the Westminster Kennel Club, and you could somehow get out of your cage at the airport, wouldn't you do it? I'm not saying it's the smartest move in the world, I'm just saying I understand *Vivy's* logic. *Vivy* is the daughter of *Chelsea Long Kiss Goodnight SC* and *Bohem All.* Doesn't sound like the kind of girl prize winner that would enjoy hanging out in a cage.

Authorities are looking for *Vivy* all over the 4,900 acre Kennedy International Airport in New York, and, of course, I hope they find her. As we've seen on endless award shows when you win something you tend to go a little nuts. In that regard dogs evidently aren't that different, particularly if your name is *Bohem C'est La Vie.*

I don't know if it's *every* airline, but a friend of mine, his wife and their little dog were going to fly on an airline that has a rule – no dogs except seeing eye or what is known as a comfort dog. As I understand it, a comfort dog is a dog without whom a passenger would be put under unacceptable stress. A letter from a psychiatrist was produced, so my friend's wife could have her little comfort dog with her.

When they checked in, more than person from the airline eyed them with a dubious look. I wonder how many little comfort dogs are flying around up there in their owner's open carry on at their feet *without a psychiatrist's letter*. After all, they wouldn't set off a metal detector, and this particular little comfort dog goes everywhere, restaurants etc. and you just about never know she's there.

If you've got a little quiet comfort dog, I hope you get to take it with you *wherever* you go in the air or on the ground. These days it's hard to imagine anyone having *too* much comfort.

It's interesting what some people study. The Oslo Natural History Museum says they have documentation on gay or lesbian behavior among whales, giraffes, penguins, parrots, and dozens of other creatures. I can see where you could spot gay or lesbian behavior among the whales, giraffes, penguins and parrots. I guess you could spot that, if you're looking for it, but they also spotted gay or lesbian behavior among beetles and even bees.

Bees, particularly I would think you'd have to keep a really sharp eye out. Bees or *beetles* it would seem particularly tough to spot gay or lesbian behavior.

Anyway because of all of this they've concluded human homosexuality cannot be viewed as "unnatural." Since there's got to be millions of gays or lesbians all over the world, who feel their sexuality *is natural* to them, I'm not positive about the need for the study in the first place. I wonder if a heterosexual bee would put down a gay bee the way some humans do to gays.

I was waiting in my car at a red light recently when I saw two identical looking dogs on a lawn by a house. One was barking its head off, and the other was staring at the barking dog and then looking out at the road seemingly thinking "Am I missing something?"

It reminded me of couples where one is *always* complaining, and the other is wondering what's going on? I'm not saying complaining is *always* wrong, but sometimes like the silent dog – let's give it a rest.

This comes under the heading of no good deed goes unpunished. My friend Henry Schleiff, who runs one of the divisions of *The Discovery Channel*, was walking a dog from a shelter in Harlem as part of a good deed day for *The Discovery Channel*.

Suddenly, from out of nowhere a pit bull jumped on the dog Henry was walking and clamped his jaws around it, as only a pit bull can. Henry desperately tried to pull his dog away, then *his* dog took quite a chomp out of *Henry's* hand. We're talking general anesthesia, endless stitches, etc. Too often – no good deed goes unpunished. That doesn't mean we shouldn't keep trying – just not around pit bulls.

Roman and Inna Flikshtein go out for a walk with their two young ones in the Manhattan Beach section in southern Brooklyn. Their thirteen-year-old daughter, Michelle, slurps a popsicle and shuffles her feet. Their youngest, Cookie, lopes behind in her red miniskirt, nibbling a peanut and dragging her knuckles on the sidewalk. Cookie is a monkey. She is a

Cercopithicus Diana, an endangered species in need of special care. State officials, after a long court battle, recently won permission to take Cookie from the Flikshteins and place her in an animal rescue program at the Detroit Zoo.

According to an article in the New York Times, Mrs. Flikshtein with tears in her eyes asked, "So what if Cookie is a monkey? She's part of this family. They want to take the baby from the mother, but she will die without us, and we will die if we give her up."

The Flikshtein's daughter Michelle refers to Cookie as her sister. The Flikshteins had argued that Cookie had adjusted enough to the human condition to spend the evenings eating ice cream and watching the evening news. Mrs. Flikshtein said her dream has always been to own a monkey.

They bought Cookie from an exotic pet store in 1995 for $4,500 and successfully toilet trained her. Dr. Shirley McGreal, Chairwoman of the International Primate Protection League in Sommerville, South Carolina said, "If I were that monkey, I'd really want to join the other monkeys in the Detroit Zoo. Monkeys know they are not people." Of course, the Flikshteins could have said people know that they are not monkeys, and yet Dr. McGreal is *sure*, if she was a monkey she'd want to go to Detroit.

Another monkey expert, Kathi Travers, spent a week living with Cookie and the Flikshteins and feels Cookie is much better off in Brooklyn with the Flikshteins than Detroit with the monkeys.

I saw this story some time ago, and it stays in my mind, because the more I look around and see how much trouble people seem to have getting along with each other, I'm starting to think that maybe we should be looking more toward different species for companionship. Add monkeys to dogs, cats, fish, birds, certainly a horse if you have the land, a cow… I definitely think it's worth looking for compatibility elsewhere.

What? Tell my parrot I'll call him back.

* * * *

ABOUT THE AUTHOR

Charles Grodin is a recipient of the William Kuntsler Award for Racial Justice and has been honored by Habitat for Humanity for his humanitarian efforts on behalf of the homeless. He is best known for his starring roles in *The Heartbreak Kid*, *Midnight Run* and the *Beethoven* movies, among others. He has written seven books including the bestseller *It Would Be So Nice If You Weren't Here*. Charles Grodin was a commentator for 60 Minutes II and is currently a commentator for CBS News. He also writes a weekly op-ed column for the New York Daily News website.

CPSIA information can be obtained
at www.ICGtesting.com
Printed in the USA
BVHW040734120519
548048BV00020B/473/P

9 780970 449993